FIRST WINTER
ON THE
EASTERN FRONT

FIRST WINTER ON THE EASTERN FRONT

1941–1942

MICHAEL OLIVE
ROBERT EDWARDS
Foreword by Chris Evans

STACKPOLE
BOOKS

Copyright © 2013 by Stackpole Books

Published in 2013 by
STACKPOLE BOOKS
5067 Ritter Road
Mechanicsburg, PA 17055
www.stackpolebooks.com

Cover design by Caroline M. Stover

Printed in the United States of America

10 9 8 7 6 5 4 3 2 1

Library of Congress Cataloging-in-Publication Data

Olive, Michael.
  First winter on the Eastern Front, 1941–1942 / Michael Olive and Robert Edwards ;
with a foreword by Chris Evans.
      pages cm. — (Stackpole military photo series)
    Includes bibliographical references.
  ISBN 978-0-8117-1125-8
  1. World War, 1939–1945—Campaigns—Eastern Front. 2. World War, 1939–1945—Campaigns—
Eastern Front—Pictorial works. 3. World War, 1939–1945—Campaigns—Soviet Union. 4. World War,
1939–1945—Campaigns—Soviet Union—Pictorial works. 5. Soviet Union—History—German occupation,
1941–1944. 6. Soviet Union—History—German occupation, 1941–1944—Pictorial works. I. Edwards,
Robert. II. Title.
  D764.O44 2013
  940.54'217—dc23
                                                    2013011946

CONTENTS

FOREWORD

In May 1942, German *Führer* Adolf Hitler authorized the awarding of the Eastern Front Medal to all German combatants and foreign volunteers who served and fought in Russia between November 15, 1941, and April 15, 1942—the first winter. The inherent irony in this is that the medal was never meant to exist. That it did meant Hitler, and Germany as a whole, had to accept a harsh new reality. Josef Stalin's Bolshevik Russia had not, as Hitler predicted—and promised—come crashing to the ground when Germany launched Operation Barbarossa, the invasion of Russia, on June 22, 1941. If anything, the resilience of the Red Army presaged that many more winters of combat lay ahead.

Made of zinc and hung by a rayon ribbon of red, black, and white, the Eastern Front Medal is plain and far from rare: over 3,000,000 were awarded during the course of the war. Printed with the simple phrase *Winterschlacht Im Osten 1941/1942* ("Winter Battle in the East"), the medal quickly received a nickname born from the gallow's humor of those who survived the frigid horrors of that first winter—*Gefrierfleischorden,* the "Frozen Meat Medal."

The German soldiers who fought in Russia in that first winter little expected the hardships they were to endure. The decisive land battles of 1939 and 1940, while not without cost, had gone so well and so quickly that they had every reason to believe in their *Führer*'s supreme confidence as they prepared to follow in Napoleon's footsteps and march to Moscow. *Blitzkrieg,* both in myth and reality, had lived up to and even surpassed its reputation. Bolshevik Russia would surely succumb as had the others, from Poland to France. The immense size and tenacity of the Red Army, the vast distances to be covered, and especially the weather would quickly put that confidence to the test.

After rapid and startling success in the opening months of Operation Barbarossa that saw the *Wehrmacht* gallop ever eastward, the invasion faltered. Russian resistance increased, coupled with a stream of reinforcements not anticipated by the *Wehrmacht.* German forces—many now more than 1,000 kilometers from their starting points—and their supplies were exhausted, and badly in need of rest, repairs, and reinforcements. Grinding the advance down even further was the beginning of the autumn rains, which turned the dirt roads into valleys of mud.

And then the ground froze, and it began to snow. With the spires of the Kremlin in Moscow visible in the distance, by December 5 the *Wehrmacht* had nonetheless managed to march to within ten kilometers of the Russian capital. With the chance to lop off the head of the Bolshevik beast in the Germans' sight, Stalin launched his counteroffensive, halting further advancement by the Germans. Reluctantly accepting that his forces could go no farther and fearing a repeat of Napoleon's disastrous retreat from Moscow, Hitler issued a directive to go on the defensive. Lacking enough food, ammunition, supplies, and winter clothing, the *Wehrmacht* would now have to stand and fight both a rejuvenated Red Army and a bitter winter in order to survive until the spring.

Michael Olive and Robert Edwards join forces once more to give the reader a detailed view of the harrowing ordeal of that first, brutal winter on the Eastern Front. Using hundreds of photographs, many never before published, they illustrate the brutal conditions and the men and weapons that fought in them.

Chris Evans
Editor
Stackpole Books

INTRODUCTION

The invasion of the Soviet Union by German forces on 22 June 1941 appeared to be an unprecedented success. The attack completely surprised the Soviets, and the front of 3,200 kilometers was ripped wide open. The Soviet forces on the border were badly deployed defensively and, except in a few instances, quickly overrun. The Germans advanced rapidly, forming massive pockets of trapped Soviet forces at Bialystock, Minsk, and Smolensk, taking literally millions of prisoners.

Initially, it seemed as if the campaign would be concluded swiftly, but the resilience of the Soviets and the effect of the vast distances on the transport of reinforcements and essential supplies—as well as the wear and tear on vehicles—were critically underestimated. The Soviet transport system was extremely primitive, with few paved roads, only one major highway from Minsk to Moscow, and a relatively sparse rail network that was of a different gauge than that of the German railways and had to be converted.

Although the Germans had won significant victories, they were still suffering casualties at an increasing rate, and replacements did not equal losses. Against the advice of his *panzer* group commanders, who pressed for an immediate assault on Moscow in July, Hitler diverted Guderian's *Panzergruppe* 2 to assist Rundstedt's Army Group South in securing the Ukraine and the Crimea. Not only was Moscow a politically pres-

tigious target, but it was a vital transport and communications hub. Another huge pocket was created at Kiev and Marshal Budenny's Southwest Group all but totally destroyed—but still the Soviet forces stubbornly fought on. The drive on Moscow was inexplicably, and ultimately fatally, delayed for nearly two months as the German High Command appeared to be unable to make a firm decision about their next objective.

Finally, on 6 September 1941, *Führer* Directive 35 was issued regarding the continuation of the war on the Eastern Front. The main objective was the elimination of the so-called "Timoshenko Army Group" operating on the Central Front. This army group was to be destroyed before the onset of winter conditions as a prerequisite for the advance on Moscow

In order to accomplish this task, all the available forces of the *Wehrmacht* and *Luftwaffe* that could be spared from the flanks were to be concentrated in the Army Group Center sector. The operation was given the cover name *Taifun* ("Typhoon"), and the attack was to begin at the earliest possible moment and was therefore planned for the end of September.

The attack was to be led by *Panzergruppe* 2 (renamed 2nd *Panzer* Army on 6 October), commanded by Germany's most dynamic tank general, Heinz Guderian. The German offensive commenced on 30 September, spearheaded by 48th *Panzer* Corps, 24th *Panzer* Corps, and 47th

Panzer Corps advancing toward Orel and Bryansk. The Soviet command was taken completely by surprise. By 1 October, the Soviet front line was shattered, and by 4 October, the 4th *Panzer* Division was at Orel, an important road and rail center. One hundred thousand gallons of fuel were supplied by air to keep the advance moving at top speed. The Soviet air force was very active, continuously bombing and strafing the advancing German columns.

On 6 October, the 4th *Panzer* Division was attacked by considerable numbers of T-34s and it was apparent that this tank was vastly superior to those of the Germans. It was faster, more maneuverable, more heavily armored, and equipped with a deadly, high-velocity 76.2mm main gun. It was only through superior tactics and cooperation with artillery, *Flak*, and *Luftwaffe* units that the *panzer* divisions could continue to advance. In an ominous portent of things to come, the first snow of winter fell, and the roads deteriorated markedly.

In the Vyazma area, the 4th and 9th Armies encircled some forty-five Soviet divisions and brigades. The 18th *Panzer* Division, in conjunction with the 43rd Army Corps of the 2nd Army, encircled three Soviet armies north of Bryansk. In these double-encirclement battles, Army Group Center claimed 673,000 prisoners, 3,500 guns, and 1,200 guns destroyed or captured. Eight Soviet armies comprising seventy-five infantry and cavalry divisions and thirteen armored divisions/brigades had been destroyed. However, on 9 October, considerable Soviet forces broke out of encirclement at Sisemka.

The stubborn defense of these pockets seriously delayed the German offensive toward Moscow. Although the encircled forces surrendered on 17 October, counterattacks from the northeast continued, and it was not until 25 October that the battles around Bryansk were considered to be over. Distinguished Soviet Marshal Georgi Zhukov acknowledged that the Germans failed to seize the capital in part because of the bravery and self-sacrifice of the troops surrounded at Vyazma.[1]

On 12 October, *OKH*[2] issued a directive for the encirclement of Moscow by the 2nd *Panzer* Army from the south and the 4th Army with *Panzergruppe* 4 from the west and north. By now, the roads were a quagmire, severely hampering operations. The supply vehicles were suited to Western European conditions and could barely move on the primitive Russian dirt roads. The supply lines were long and ever more tenuous due to increased partisan activity, with supply trains being attacked and rail lines sabotaged. As a result, adequate supplies could not be brought up to the advancing troops. Astonishingly, no planning had been made for winter warfare. Heavy-weight winter lubricants were not available, and both vehicles and weapons increasingly ceased to function. In many instances, fires had to be lit under truck and armored vehicle engines to thaw the almost frozen oil. Even more seriously, the frontline troops lacked adequate winter clothing, and the first instances of frostbite were being reported.

On 29 October, *OKH* ordered the drive on Moscow to begin as soon as weather conditions permitted—with the muddy roads frozen and therefore more passable. The 2nd *Panzer* Army was tasked with capturing Gorki, which was 640 kilometers east of Moscow, so as to isolate the Russian capital from its rearward communications. Given the weather, the condition of the troops, and the numerous vehicle breakdowns, this was an impossible task. These orders were an indication that both *OKH* and *OKW*[3] were far removed from the realities of what was actually happening at the front. The *panzer* divisions were

1. G. K. Zhukov, *Marshal Zhukov's Greatest Battles* (London: Macdonald, 1969).

2. *Oberkommando des Heeres*—High Command of the Armed Forces.

3. *Oberkommando der Wehrmacht*—High Command of the Army (ground forces).

now at around 35 percent of their authorized strength.

A report on 17 November indicated that fresh troops were arriving on the battlefield, with Siberian troops being identified in the Vslovia sector. General Georgi Zhukov, who had been responsible for the successful defense of Leningrad, was summoned to Supreme Soviet Headquarters on 1 November to assume responsibility for the command of the Western Front and the defense of Moscow. General Zhukov was experienced, an exceptional planner and strategist—and absolutely ruthless in achieving his military aims. Zhukov correctly identified the main axis of the German advance and deployed his troops accordingly. Barely trained reinforcements were being rushed to the front along with veteran troops from the East. Of the thirty-four fresh divisions that arrived on the Western Front, twenty-one were committed against Army Group Center. Numerous "Workers Brigades" were being formed in Moscow to defend the city, and the civilian population was mobilized on a massive scale to construct extensive defensive belts around the city.

The German offensive ground on in appalling conditions, with barely adequate supplies, particularly fuel, getting to the troops. There was no question of making sweeping envelopments as had been the case in the earlier encirclement battles; costly frontal attacks were the only option. The 14th *Panzer* Corps of the 2nd *Panzer* Army, reinforced with Infantry Regiment *Grossdeutschland,* advanced on Tula, a communications center and airfield essential for the continued advance on Moscow, but the city could not be taken. The Soviet troops were no longer surrendering *en masse* but fighting to the last man.

The eastern flank of the 2nd *Panzer* Army was now badly exposed. Guderian advised the commander of Army Group Center, Field Marshal Bock, that the offensive could not be con-

tinued, but with no result. By 30 November, total German casualties on the Eastern Front since the beginning of the campaign reached a staggering total of 743,000, which was 23 percent of the average troop strength of three and a half million men. Of the twenty-six goods trains that were required daily to deliver even the minimum supply requirements, only eight to ten were eventually getting through.

In the north, the offensive toward Leningrad had bogged down, and Army Group North had failed to link up with Finnish forces to complete the encirclement of the city. Army Group South had captured the important city of Rostov on 21 November. However, Soviet forces counterattacked on 28 November, and on 30 November, Rostov was evacuated by Army Group South. Field Marshal Rundstedt was relieved of his command for ordering a retreat, a harbinger of things to come. It was only in the center of the front that any progress was being made, albeit slowly and at a high cost.

Bock reported to *OKH* on 1 December that "In heavy fighting the attack will probably result in limited territorial gains, and enemy forces will certainly be destroyed, but any strategic results are very unlikely."[4] He requested that the attack be broken off and a defensible line occupied. By now, relations between Hitler and the High Command were at a low ebb. Hitler was convinced of his own strategic abilities and increasingly distrusted the members of his General Staff.

Despite his considerable misgivings, Guderian launched his attack to encircle Moscow on 2 December with the 24th *Panzer* Corps. Initially, the attack was successful, but by 6 December, it had stalled with units of Reinhardt's 3rd Army within twenty miles of the Kremlin.

With the troops exhausted and suffering severely from the coldest winter in years, temper-

---

4. H. A. Jacobsen and J. Rohwer, eds., *Decisive Battles of World War II: The German View* (London: Andre Deutsch Limited, 1965).

atures of -30 Centigrade (-22F) were recorded in December, the Germans no longer had the resources to continue the advance. A phased withdrawal to a prepared position—the Susha-Oka position—that had been partially fortified in October was the only sensible course of action.

The canny Zhukov held his nerve, and when the German advance ground to a halt, his Western Front and the Kalinin Front under General Koniev commenced offensive operations with masses of well-equipped troops and tanks. The main focus was against 2nd *Panzer* Army near Venez, *Panzer* Group 3 on the Moscow Canal, and the right wing of the 9th Army near Kalinin.

Due to the weather and road conditions, the German units could not retreat for more than a few kilometers at a time without losing considerable quantities of equipment, in particular artillery and vehicles. The retreating columns were continually attacked from the flanks, and the rearguards faced unceasing pressure. *Panzergruppe* 3 and 4 were continually in danger of being encircled. There were no longer any reserves available to shore up the front. Initially, Hitler refused to approve any withdrawals regardless of the circumstances. After days of seemingly fruitless arguing, the army group was finally given some freedom of action, and it immediately ordered that a line Kursk–Orel–Medyn–Rzhev was to be prepared as a winter position to fall back on. On 10 December, it was announced that a number of divisions were to be transferred from the West, but due to the chaotic rail situation, these units would not arrive for several weeks.

Hitler's infamous "No Retreat" order, insisting that his soldiers offer fanatical resistance to the enemy, was issued on 16 December. No major withdrawals were to be made until the reserves were in place in the prepared positions in the rear. This was unlikely to inspire confidence in the frontline troops. Prior to this order being issued, Guderian ordered the withdrawal of his 2nd *Panzer* Army to a line behind the Plava River, almost certainly saving it from encirclement and subsequent destruction.

The crisis for the Germans continued both on the battlefield and at army headquarters as on 19 December Field Marshal Brauchitsch resigned as commander in chief of the army due to a heart complaint. Hitler did not replace him but personally assumed command of the army. Also on the 19, Bock was sacked, being replaced by Field Marshal Kluge. General Guderian, in defiance of Hitler's express order, initiated a further withdrawal of 2nd *Panzer* Army to the Suscha-Oka position on 25 December. That same day, he was removed from his command, and the commander of 2nd Army, General Rudolf Schmidt, who was not known as an expert in the employment of armored forces, was given command of 2nd *Panzer* Army.

Initially, the aim of the Soviet High Command was the destruction of the two armored groups threatening Moscow. The ultimate aim, however, was the envelopment and destruction of Army Group Center. Soviet tactics consisted of continuous attacks by both large and small formations all along the front, usually preceded by massive artillery barrages. Most of these attacks broke down in the face of a desperate German resistance with heavy casualties being sustained on both sides. However, this continuous pressure prevented the Germans from massing any reserves and sending them to the most threatened areas of the front. A large gap formed between the 2nd *Panzer* Army and the 4th Army, and the Soviets poured the 50th Army, reinforced by three cavalry divisions, into that gap. By 20 December, the situation was critical as a Soviet breakthrough at the vital transport hub at Orel was imminent. There was now only loose contact between Army Group North and Army Group Center. Twenty-two Soviet infantry divisions and five armored brigades attacked eight weak German divisions at Livny and Verkhov. The 2nd *Panzer* Army and the 2nd Army withdrew to a line west of Tim-Mtsensk and south of Belev—the Winter Position—and succeeded in holding it despite enormous pressure.

The Soviet attempt at a breakthrough at Orel was repulsed but the intent was still to take the southern wing of the 4th Army in a pincer movement by driving on Yukhov. The gap between the 4th Army and the 2nd *Panzer* Army was now some sixty-five kilometers wide, and the 40th *Panzer* Corps was thrown in to the gap to stop the seemingly inexorable Soviet advance. Both flanks of the 4th Army were no longer in contact with other German forces, but Hitler insisted that there be no retreat and encirclement now seemed inevitable.

By the end of December, *Panzergruppe* 3 and 4 faced three Soviet armies but had managed to stabilize the front in the Ruza and Lama sectors, but the situation was still extremely dangerous as the two *panzer* groups were now effectively immobilized due to deep snow and a lack of fuel.

January brought the Germans no respite from the continuous crises on all sectors of the front, and the temperature continued to plummet. There was now only a tenuous link between the 9th Army and Army Group North, but as usual, Hitler refused permission for the 9th Army to fall back on the Winter Line.

On 2 January, the German front in the Rzhev area was broken, and the two main focal points of the Soviet offensive became clear as it was at those points that the Soviets now massed the majority of their forces. The southern point was the drive to Vyazma and Smolensk, and the northern point was the cracking open of the 9th Army boundary and the execution of a deadly enveloping movement in the rear of that army.

The overwhelming superiority of fresh, well-equipped troops against a badly extended German front, held by exhausted, inadequately supplied troops, presaged a major disaster. On

all fronts, there was a critical shortage of infantry and no reserves to speak of. The northern flank of 2nd *Panzer* Army was threatened with envelopment, and both flanks of the 4th *Panzer* Army were also threatened with envelopment. The commander of 4th *Panzer* Army, General Hoepner, ordered a withdrawal in order to avoid encirclement and was summarily dismissed by Hitler.

General Zhukov wanted to direct the main Soviet offensive against Army Group Center as he, quite correctly, calculated that it was in this sector that the greatest possibility of a major encirclement existed. However, Stalin, as interfering in day-to-day operations as was Hitler, directed that the offensive be mounted all along the front. Zhukov's concerns that there were not enough troops or armored vehicles to accomplish more than local successes in the north and south were summarily dismissed, and to make matters worse, on the 19 January, the 1st Shock Army was transferred to the reserve pool. Coupled with the transfer of the 13th Army to the Kalinin Front on 16 December, the offensive power of the right flank of the Western Front was seriously compromised.

Both the German frontline commanders and their troops were by now almost at breaking point due to the anxieties caused by the incessant and enormous Soviet pressure. The Soviet forces were streaming through the gap between the two army groups at Ostashkov and continuous stress was being exerted at the breakthrough points at Sukhinichi and Rzhev. As Zhukov had planned, Army Group Center was once again in real danger of encirclement in the Vyazma area. German reserves were still non-existent, and by the time the reserves finally arrived from the West, it would be too late. The only possibility of both accumulating reserves and averting disaster was to shorten the front line.

Finally, on 15 January, after weeks of pointless argument and vacillation, the center of the front was given permission to conduct a fighting withdrawal to the Winter Line on the condition that the gap between 4th Army and 4th *Panzer* Army be closed. This condition was not able to be achieved and the withdrawal commenced despite the perilously open flanks. The 2nd Army was placed under the command of Army Group South in order to secure the southern flank of Army Group Center.

On 15 January, Army Group Center gave the order to abandon the salients at Kaluga (4th Army), Rusa (4th *Panzer* Army) and Volokolamsk (3rd *Panzer* Army) and withdraw to the Winter Line from 18 to 24 January. Despite these orders, in the following weeks, the continuing Soviet attacks upset the German plans almost completely. The situation was always critical and the threat of encirclement always present.

The gap between the army groups was now some 100 kilometers wide. The Soviet 3rd Shock Army was driving on Velikiye-Luki, and the 4th Shock Army was rapidly advancing toward Velizh and Demidov. Four German infantry divisions— the 246th, 83rd, 330th, and 205th, respectively— were committed and helped to stabilize the situation.

The Soviet 33rd Army exploited the gap between the 4th Army and 4th *Panzer* Army and advanced toward Yukhnov. The Germans scraped together sufficient forces to counter-attack from the north and south in an attempt to seal off the breakthrough, but the German forces could get no closer than ten kilometers from each other. However, the Soviets were not able to continue the advance, and parts of the 33rd Army and some cavalry units massed behind German lines in a heavily forested area, joining with both airborne troops that had been dropped in the area since 18 January and substantial numbers of partisans.

On 24 January, the Soviet 61st Army broke through to the south in the rear of the 53rd Army Corps, but that dangerous advance was halted the next day as yet another impending catastrophe was averted. The German defense lines held firm with the Soviet forces now battering themselves to destruction against the "hedgehog-style" defenses based on towns and villages. The Soviet troops were now as exhausted as their German counterparts, having suffered exceptionally heavy losses in both men and equipment.

By early February, the German commanders considered the situation stabilized and were now confident that with the arrival of substantial reinforcements during the month, the danger of further breakthroughs was minimal.

The Soviets had achieved a significant defensive success, preventing the capture of Moscow and advancing more than 240 kilometers in some instances. There were, however, no large-scale encirclements and the subsequent destruction of large numbers of German troops.

In the case of the Germans, there was no repeat of Napoleon's disastrous retreat from Moscow and the subsequent destruction of his army in 1812. The Soviets threw 117 new divisions into the battle in marked contrast to the Germans, who were reinforced with a meager 9 divisions. The Germans held almost all of their vital communication centers such as Schlüsselburg, Novgorod, Rzhev, Vyazma, Bryansk, Orel, Kursk, Kharkov, and Taganrog. These "fortresses" were vital barriers for both tactical and also strategic reasons as they were focal points of the sparse network of communications. The Soviets could not be prevented from infiltrating into the open spaces between these bastions, but their failure to capture them meant that their advance was severely compromised and the German salients thereby formed provided excellent jumping off points for the summer offensive operations.

It has been contended that Hitler's insistence on no retreat under any circumstances was the correct strategic decision and largely responsible for preventing a catastrophe. Although the destruction of the German ground forces was ultimately avoided and the Soviet offensive blunted, this is not of itself sufficient evidence that Hitler's order was responsible for the defensive success. In actuality, the insistence on holding onto ground no matter what the odds or the cost almost certainly caused more casualties than a measured withdrawal would have.

The army and divisional commanders were denied a freedom of action that would have allowed them to more effectively respond to the rapidly changing circumstances. There was no widespread call by commanders for a lengthy retreat by all the defending formations as it was recognized that this was not feasible and to do so would have invited encirclement and ultimately destruction. Rather, as a result of small tactical withdrawals, some lines could have been shortened, reducing the vast areas that the understrength formations were defending and allowing the creation of reserves. The Winter Line was only some eighty kilometers behind the front line and closer to the vital supply lines, particularly the rail heads.

The savage winter battles were, in fact, a tribute to the courage and determination of both sides. That the Soviets could mount such a large-scale offensive after suffering such massive casualties since 22 June was remarkable. For the outnumbered and inadequately supplied Germans to contain the Soviet offensive in such appalling and unfamiliar conditions was a prodigious feat of arms.

A general map of the Eastern Front from 5 December 1941 to 30 April 1942 showing the limit of the German advance and the gains made by the Soviet counterattack. The creation of several awkward salients is evident. Both the Germans and Soviets intended to use these salients to resume the offensive as soon as the ground hardened.

THE INFANTRY

A lone sentry stands guard over a partially destroyed Russian town. When on the defensive, the Germans made extensive use of these localities, fortified to whatever degree was possible, to slow down or halt the threatening Soviet advances.

Mountain troops, identified by their leggings, jackets, and peaked cloth caps (*Bergmütze*), construct a makeshift command post.

A makeshift hut constructed with blocks of ice, complete with a heater.

Soldiers watch as a village hut burns to the ground. Since the shovels indicate they were trying to put it out or at least contain it, the fire was probably in a hut the soldiers were also using as quarters. Under the brutal winter conditions suffered that first winter on the Eastern Front, the fighting often centered around capturing built-up areas and denying the same to the enemy. The future prospect for the civilian family is grim at best.

Another view of the same scene with a horse-drawn supply trailer in the foreground.

While the motorcycle gave the Germans tremendous advantages along the good road networks of Western Europe, they were frequently hampered by the atrocious road conditions encountered in the Soviet Union, especially during inclement weather. The motorcycle messengers and the motorcycle infantry units—*Kradschützen*—often made better progress dismounted. Of interest in these two images is the wearing of the special motorcyclist's rubberized jacket, intended to help keep the messengers dry on their travels. In the second image, one of the motorcyclists is having his feet rubbed by a comrade in an effort to increase circulation and prevent frostbite.

Mail call! Given the primitive conditions of the Eastern Front, one of the few pleasures the soldiers could enjoy was correspondence and packages from home. With the exception of one soldier, everyone is bundled warmly in an oftentimes unsuccessful effort to combat the cold. The other pleasure was the opportunity to receive warm rations. In the front lines, soldiers frequently had to forego a hot meal. Even if efforts were made to provide them, by the time they arrived at the front in sub-zero weather, they were frequently cold, if not frozen.

Artillery observers manning a forward observation post.

General and field-grade officers visit units at the front. It was usual *Wehrmacht* practice for higher-grade officers to keep in close contact with their frontline units. These officers often became casualties. Unfortunately, the higher command totally lost touch with realities at the front and placed demands on the soldiers that could not met.

According to Heinz Guderian in his *Panzer Leader*, "The icy cold, the lack of shelter, the shortage of clothing, the heavy losses of men and equipment, the wretched state of our fuel supplies—all this makes the duties of a commander a misery, and the longer it goes on, the more I am crushed by the enormous responsibility which I have to bear, a responsibility which no one, even with the best will in the world, can share."

Although hard to identify, this photo may be of the *Führer*, Adolf Hitler. If this is the case, it was not taken anywhere near the Eastern Front, as Hitler directed the war from headquarters in Berlin or East Prussia, far behind the front lines. The total lack of appreciation by the higher command for the conditions at the front was a constant source of anger and frustration for the frontline commanders.

An infantry squad prepares to move out. The heavy piece of equipment carried by the soldier at the front indicates that this is not a just patrol, but a move to a forward position.

One of those forward positions: an entrenchment.

Another group portrait, this time next to a *Gulaschkanone*—"Goulash cannon"—as the soldiers referred to the horse-drawn mobile field mess kitchens. These men seem to be well equipped for the cold, as evidenced by the winter boots, overcoats, and an assortment of earmuffs and toques. The caps still have the branch coloring present on the front as part of the insignia. It appears to be white, denoting infantry, but it is not always possible to ascertain the exact color in gray-scale images. The soutache material was removed in 1942 in a cost-cutting measure. The soldier smoking appears to be a medic, as evidenced by the partial view of the armband, which would have had a red cross on it.

Rations arrive at the front. The provision of hot food to the troops was a high priority. However, keeping it warm was extremely difficult. By the time the food was delivered to the battlefront, it was frequently frozen solid.

A small Russian village occupied by German troops. It appears that some windbreaks have been set up around the huts.

This squad has the relative luxury of being transported by truck, even if it is open, rather than slogging through the snow. (The clothing seems to indicate that this photograph was taken after the winter of 1941–1942.)

Various signs indicating command and administrative elements of the *6. Infanterie-Division.*

An NCO uses a megaphone to relay orders—or perhaps the soldiers are just horsing around. The cylinders appear to be air-dropped supply containers.

Posing in front of a typical Russian thatched hut. Two of the soldiers wear the highly desired felt boots, which provided excellent protection against the cold. Numerous captured Soviet factories produced these boots for the German Army; in many instances, boots were taken from Soviet dead and prisoners.

An impromptu officer conference on a bridge over a frozen river. Given the relaxed attitude, the front line is likely a safe distance away.

Heavily bundled up against the biting cold. The standard M1934 field cap, worn here, was not suitable for the Russian winter although the "turn up" or flap could be lowered to protect the ears. Field-grey wool toques are worn under the cap.

In the photograph above, the standard-issue greatcoat is worn with an improvised sheepskin cap and felt boots. The greatcoat was quite suitable for a European winter but inadequate for a Russian one. The felt boots were necessary as the standard leather "jackboot," with its hob-nailed sole, transmitted the cold to the soldier's feet, causing frostbite. An expedient solution was to stuff the soles and side of the boot with newspaper, which was a good insulator, at least until it became wet.

Improvised white coverings that provided a measure of camouflage in the snow. The effectiveness of the white snow suits worn by Soviet troops prompted the German troops to use whatever field-expedient items that were available to them, such as these "snow shirts."

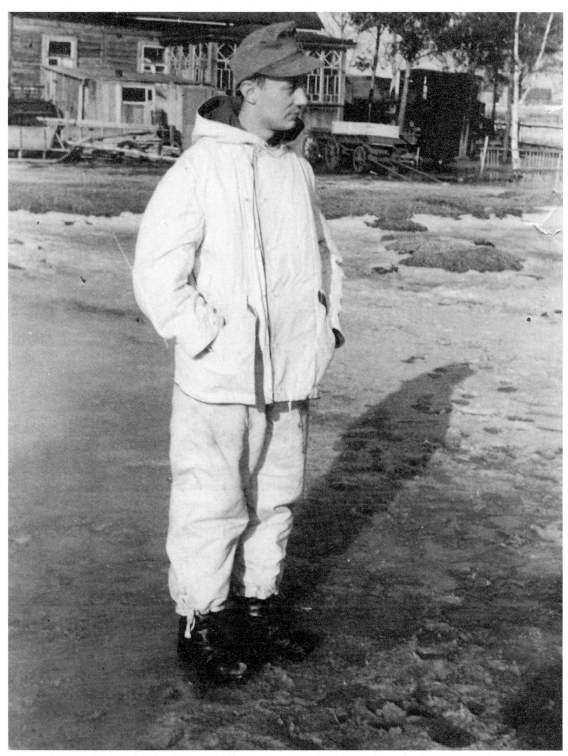

As a result of that first winter on the Eastern Front, the German armed forces eventually developed specialized clothing such as this winter suit in reversible white/mouse grey (later models were in white/camouflage). This very practical garment was designed to be worn over the standard uniform and was constructed of up to three layers of material, with the external layer being both wind- and waterproof.

Two mountain divisions saw action on the central portion of the Eastern Front during the winter of 1941–42, the *1.* and the *4. Gebirgs-Division*, which they were generally employed along the Mius. There were several other mountain divisions at the time, but most were employed in the far north in Lapland. Many of the mountain troopers seen in these images wore the *Bergmütze*, which is often mistaken for the ubiquitous M43 billed field cap, which was introduced in 1943. The mountain cap differed from the M43 inasmuch as the brim was shorter, frequently had two ventilation holes along each side, and also frequently had a distinctly lighter color wool than the typical German field gray.

The symbol of the mountain trooper, the *Edelweiß* (a mountain flower of the sunflower family), can be seen on the right sleeves above.

A Finnish soldier on guard with a Maxim machine gun. Finnish doctrine used the machine gun much like artillery, firing it at great distances to disrupt infantry attacks.

A more typical image associated with the *Gebirgsjäger*, operations in a mountainous region.

Soldiers pull guard. When the weather turned especially cold, guard posts usually had a minimum of two soldiers manning them so that they could keep an eye on each other, especially for signs of frostbite. As opposed to a normal one- or two-hour rotation, guards frequently had to be changed out every thirty minutes or less. In addition to the normal duties of protecting the perimeter, guards often had to start engines at regular intervals and check other mechanical devices to see whether they had frozen up.

An impressive snow cave serves as a backdrop for a photograph for family members at home or perhaps for propaganda purposes. No amount of propaganda could hide the fact that things were not going as planned on the Eastern Front during the winter of 1941–42. Soldiers' letters home became increasingly pessimistic.

Finland proved to be Germany's most capable ally on the Eastern Front, and for good reason: Finnish soldiers were skilled in winter-warfare and had already fought the much larger Red Army to a draw concluded by the Moscow Peace Treaty in the winter of 1939–40.

Another example of an improvised white coverall and helmet cover. Also visible is what appears to be a type of fur collar.

Just how effective at camouflage the white snow smocks were is evident from this photograph. These smocks look like they are manufactured rather than field-expedient items (they may be regulation issue to mountain troops). The colored armbands are for unit identification.

Waiting for the enemy: a shallow dugout well supplied with weapons, including rifles, hand grenades, and machine-gun magazines. The soldier in the foreground seems to be wearing a mountain-troops cap.

An air guard maintains a lonely vigil outside a village. Machine guns intended for aerial defense in rearward areas were usually positioned in the open to allow the gunners a free field of fire for their weapons. Note the aerial sight mounted on the barrel of the *MG 13/15*.

Soldiers move in single file through a cut in the woods. This might be an infantry heavy weapons section, since one of the soldiers is carrying a base plate for a mortar.

Field-expedient white smocks worn by a machine-gun squad.

The vastness and desolation of the Russian winter landscape is evident here. The enormous distances and unfamiliar landscapes of the Eastern Front had a profound psychological effect on the German soldier. In the words of *Landser* Claus Hansmann (as quoted in Stephen G. Fritz's *Frontsoldaten*): "And then winter: frost, brutal cold, raging icy wind, snowstorms and snow, shrouding everything, white, broad expanses on which only the wind draws noteworthy figures. Snow-covered villages, loneliness."

Field-made white helmet covers offer little camouflage when worn with the field grey uniform.

The same group of soldiers man an entrenchment defending the village hut they are probably living in. The winter campaign often became desperate small-unit actions fighting for shelter.

Large tracts of the Soviet Union were covered in dense forest unsuitable for swiftly moving armored operations. As the partisan movement became more widespread, these areas became hiding places for literally thousands of regular troops that were cut off from the front line and civilians resisting the German occupation of their homeland.

The sign says it all: "Individual vehicles stop! Danger of partisans in the woods. Wait for vehicles following you to cross the woods together!"

A forward observer uses the wreckage of an aircraft as cover. The order to stand fast and not retreat at least eliminated uncertainty in the mind of the soldiers, as explained by *Leutnant* F. Wilhelm Christians in Robert J. Kershaw's *War without Garlands*: "Don't ask me if we complained, or if we had a mind of our own. What remained for us to do? There was no freedom of action, or indeed the idea of it! Nobody debated whether he would participate! Such issues were never raised. We were given a mission and we took orders seriously."

Tents were used to provide some protection from the cold but were only effective if provided with some form of heating, as in this instance.

Collecting firewood for the stove of this well-constructed hut. Unfortunately, many of these huts were infected with lice, the bane of the German soldier on the Eastern Front and spreader of dreaded typhus. Of interest are the clumsy woven straw boots, warm but severely restricting mobility.

Wool-lined caps complete with national insignia worn with a non-regulation knitted scarf and turtleneck sweater. The strict uniform regulations were essentially ignored during the initial winter on the Eastern Front, with a large variety of civilian items worn.

Another view of a supply convoy: in this instance, the supply wagons are standard-issue light supply trailers for horse-drawn supply columns. These horses are larger than the *panje* ponies and therefore able to pull heavier loads.

In November 1941 Guderian wrote: "We are only nearing our final objective step by step in the icy cold and with all the troops suffering from the appalling supply situation. Yet the brave troops are seizing all their advantages and are fighting with wonderful endurance despite all their handicaps. Over and over again, I am thankful that our men are such good soldiers."

A well turned out soldier in regulation-issue greatcoat and leather boots .

Not looking quite so immaculate, these soldiers are wearing white smocks over their uniforms and greatcoats. The soldier on the right is wearing the Iron Cross, Second Class, worn on a ribbon only on the day of the award.

Details of the uniform of an *Obergefreiter*. He is a recipient of the Infantry Assault Badge (*Infanteriesturmabzeichen*); the award criteria was participation in three separate actions or being wounded during one of them. In addition, he wears the ribbon for the Iron Cross, Second Class, and the Wound Badge in Black.

A busy supply dump in the middle of a forest. In order to continue their offensive operations, the Soviet troops had to rely on capturing German supply dumps, which they accomplished on many occasions. The German system of distributing supplies left much to be desired as massive amounts of clothing, food, and ammunition were stockpiled and not sent to the front line due to bureaucratic intransigence and inefficiency.

These soldiers are well protected against the cold. They are sitting on what appears to be a Soviet BA-10 armored car.

A wounded or sick soldier is carefully loaded into a wheeled field ambulance, which was known to the German soldier as a *Sanka* (*Sanitätskraftfahrwagen* = medical vehicle). The vehicle appears to have been whitewashed, and the oversized red cross may also have been covered up, since the cross frequently only served to facilitate aiming by a ruthless opponent. The interior of the doors may also have been painted white, although it is more likely the cream-colored interior color employed on most German vehicles. Note the man on the left carrying the extra blankets to help guard against the cold for the journey.

Despite the war, life must go on for these Russian villagers. In many cases, the German soldiers established good relationships with the Russian population and bartered for fresh food and lodging.

In this sequence of photos, a Finnish soldier prepares to throw a hand grenade into a crude Russian shelter and then watches it burn. Despite its overwhelming superiority in numbers of men, tanks, aircraft, and artillery, the Red Army suffered heavy losses in its short-lived war against Finland in the winter of 1939–40.

Some idea of the debilitating cold can be seen in this photograph. Usually, the soldiers covered their faces as much as possible to prevent frostbite.

German engineer units were well supplied with pneumatic boats for river crossings. The lack of steel helmets and the presence of a photographer indicates this is probably a training exercise. This training was essential due to the numerous waterways in Russia.

Officers take time to converse, perhaps prior to or following an orders conference, as indicated by the map and the different branch colors on the caps, indicating officer personnel from several different types of elements coming together. Both of the officers in the middle wear the very popular "crusher" cap, which had been introduced for field wear in 1937. By this time, it had been officially phased out, but it was so popular that it continued to be worn until the end of the war. In fact, after it became difficult to buy a *Feldmütze alter Art*, some officers took regulation visor caps, removed the chin cords, buttons, and top spring stiffener in an effort to make their caps appear like a "crusher." This was true even among some general officers. The sheepskin "collars" are an interesting method of warding off the cold.

This fortunate soldier has acquired a roughly made sheepskin coat, heavy mittens, and some sort of non-regulation hat. The usual fairly smart appearance of *Wehrmacht* units deteriorated markedly during the winter months.

The sheepskin overcoat was issued for guard and driver duty. Although ideal for the winter conditions, these garments were not widely distributed. The officer below probably purchased his coat privately.

A wide variety of somewhat roughly made jackets is on display here. All uniform regulations were suspended during the first winter—anything warm could be worn. Much was made of the National Socialist drive to collect warm clothing in Germany for distribution to the troops, but most of the clothing collected was not distributed to the troops until the worst of the winter weather was over.

A brief respite from the harsh reality of combat or a staged event for propaganda photographers?

Preparations are made for a proxy wedding, known as a *Ferntrauung*. These were enabled by Hitler on 4 November 1939 as a means to allow soldiers to marry when the frontline situation did not permit their immediate return home. The soldier would take his vows in front of an officer. In some cases, it was possible to establish communications with the home front, enabling the betrothed to actually hear the vows being exchanged. Generally, however, the ceremonies were performed only in front of the soldier's comrades from the unit. In Germany, these were often referred to as *Stahlhelmtrauungen* ("helmet weddings"), since a helmet was placed at the spot the groom would normally take during the ceremony. The soldiers in the field liked the ceremonies, especially since it was usually an occasion for a unit's first sergeant to distribute extra personal demand items, especially alcohol.

As indicated by the lack of greatcoats, the weather is relatively mild. Photographs such as these were taken to reassure family on the home front that conditions were not so bad.

Soviet prisoners trundle westward to an uncertain future. Although German policy was not intentionally neglectful of them, the sheer magnitude of captured personnel, especially in the first year of the war, overwhelmed the German capability of adequately taking care of them, especially since it was frequently unable to provide adequately for its own soldiers.

These Red Army prisoners captured by the Finnish Army had a somewhat better chance of surviving than their comrades captured by the Germans.

Enemy prisoners receive rations. Many former Soviet prisoners eventually volunteered to serve with German units, since they were generally treated as equals by the frontline soldiers and given the same food, quarters, and creature comforts as German soldiers. By midwar, German divisions had grown accustomed to having these *Hilfsfreiwillige*—referred to as *Hiwis* in German soldier slang—and their presence was even officially authorized on the German equivalent of the table of organization and equipment, the *Kriegsstärkenachweisung (KStN)*.

A well-constructed log structure that nonetheless seems a little small for the effort involved. It may be intended as some sort of bunker.

All four of these *Landser* have received the Infantry Assault Badge, the *Infanteriesturmabzeichen*. The German High Command were very aware of the morale value of awards in recognition of bravery in combat.

A machine-gun position and dugout. Once the ground was frozen, entrenching tools were useless, and positions had to be blasted out with explosives, if any were available.

A sniper camouflaged by his white anorak takes aim at a distant target. The standard German infantry weapon, the *Kar 98k* rifle, outranged the widely used Soviet PPSh-41 submachine gun. However, the Soviet weapon was far more suitable for close combat use with its ability to fire on full automatic.

Camaraderie was considered by the *Wehrmacht* to be essential in promoting combat efficiency. Friedrich Gruppe (quoted in *Frontsoldaten* by Stephen G. Fritz) wrote that he was part of "the community of those accustomed to war and those comrades sworn to each other."

An infantry squad dressed in an assortment of clothing, including what appears to be the white drill uniform made from cotton herringbone twill. The soldier on the right carries the excellent *MP 40* submachine gun.

Mountain soldiers set up two *MG 34's* on tripods.

The observers indicate that these machine guns (also seen on the previous page) were set up for training purposes. Note the mountain insignia, the *Edelweiß*, and the short-brimmed *Bergmütze* on several of the soldiers.

Mountain troops in the front line: time to put the instructions on operating the *MG 34* to good use.

A field-expedient white coverall and whitewashed helmet will help this soldier blend in with his surroundings.

A *Waffen SS* unit secures a village. Generally, the *Waffen SS* was better supplied with winter clothing than its army counterparts as the *SS* had its own manufacturing facilities and had more adequately prepared for the cold conditions.

A patrol advances through a scene of devastation. Günther von Scheven wrote of the winter battles of 1941–42 (quoted in Stephen G. Fritz's *Frontsoldaten*): "It is not possible to give an impression of those ghostly weeks."

The desolate conditions in the front lines. A machine gunner is using a blanket or a tarpaulin to keep warm and provide some concealment.

Compared to their German counterparts, their allies the Finns–much like Russian forces–were well equipped to fight in winter conditions.

Hardly a regulation jacket! Once the shortage of winter clothing became apparent, Minister for Propaganda Josef Göbbels made a great show of the Nazi Party collecting civilian winter clothing for distribution to the troops. In reality very few items of clothing made it to the troops until winter was almost over. Note the waterproofing leggings.

A sentry on the alert for a surprise attack. The Red Army pressure on both defending and retreating German forces was unrelenting. Large- and small-scale attacks, with and without preparatory artillery fire, were carried out on an almost continuous basis all along the front. Reserves were non-existent.

Motorcycle infantry in field-expedient white coveralls. The Soviet use of white snowsuits as effective camouflage prompted the Germans to do the same, using whatever material was available.

The muddy roads not only made the movement of vehicles, including tracked vehicles, exceedingly difficult, but glutinous mud stuck to boots and severely hampered the movement of infantry.

A young SS *Untersturmführer* (second lieutenant) appraises himself of the situation. The steady performance of the *Waffen SS* units during the Soviet counteroffensive impressed the Army High Command.

An *MG 34* in the heavy machine-gun role. When the lubricating oil froze, making the weapon inoperable, it was discovered that if the weapon was cleaned of oil, it could still operate without it.

SS-Division (mot.) "Reich" operating with the *1. Panzer-Division* north of Sytschewka.

Soldiers of *SS-Division "Totenkopf"* guard the perimeter of fortress Demjansk.

A machine-gun position of *SS-Division (mot.) "Reich"* in January 1942.

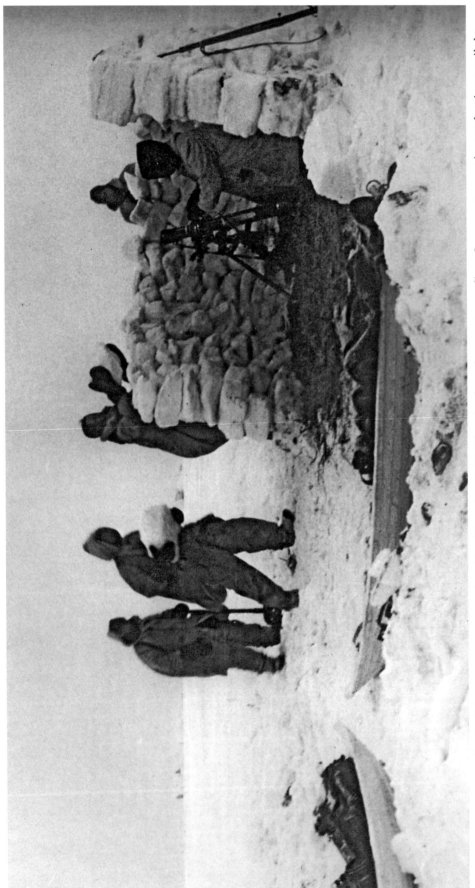

Blocks of ice being used to build a revetment around an *8cm Granatwerfer 34*. The sturdy and accurate medium 8cm mortar was in production until the end of the war. Mortars were of limited use because the effects of their high-explosive rounds were muffled by the deep snow.

Preparations for Christmas often took on elaborate trappings, if the frontline situation would allow. In a quiet(er) sector of the front, no effort was spared to give the soldier a taste of home, including distribution of extra personal demand items such as chocolate and tobacco, the preparation of a Christmas meal, and the decorating of a Christmas tree.

A simpler celebration. A group poses around a Christmas tree featuring homemade decorations. There are a few bottles of spirits and even a *Weihnachtsmann* (Santa Claus), as evidenced by the soldier with the white beard in the middle of the picture.

Numerous items used to stay warm are evident in this photograph. These include an additional overcoat worn over the greatcoat (possibly a captured Soviet item), two types of fur collar, and the overshoes made of straw. Although these overshoes provided a good deal of warmth, they were clumsy and made movement difficult. When they became wet, they fell apart.

Enlisted *Luftwaffe* personnel find time to celebrate with comrades. Due to the more permanent nature of airfields, *Luftwaffe* personnel enjoyed more comfort than the infantry.

A soldier poses with his accordion.

While opportunities for socializing were few and far between, those that presented themselves were taken advantage of. Here soldiers have some wine and listen to music in the narrow confines of their hut or dugout. Firsthand accounts are full of episodes where soldiers found phonographs and records, which soon became the highpoint of frontline existence—whenever the time was found to enjoy them.

Even at the front, Christmas trees were sometimes erected, as evidenced by this scene outside a dugout. At first glance, it would seem to be just a fir tree next to the entryway, but close examination reveals Christmas balls hanging from some of the limbs.

A lonely grave in the vast, frozen wilderness.

German soldiers had the utmost respect for fallen comrades and made every effort to identify gravesites with the name, rank, and unit of the deceased. Where possible, the bodies were transferred to mass graveyards.

Due to the frozen ground, bodies could not be buried unless explosives were used. If the bodies were not buried, there was a great risk of disease when the ground thawed.

The German Winter Line was to be anchored, as much as possible, on major rivers.

During the Finnish-Soviet War in 1940, the Finns used ski troops extensively to interdict supply lines and disrupt communications. Relatively small numbers of these ski troops created havoc behind Soviet lines. The Soviet forces also effectively used ski troops on a large scale during the winter offensive. The Germans had relatively few trained *Skijäger* and instituted training programs in an attempt to emulate the Finnish example.

This appears to be some sort of training exercise or demonstration. The instructor certainly seems to be getting his point across.

Even with skis, it was sometimes difficult to negotiate deep snow.

Captured Soviet fur caps were very popular and highly sought after by the troops. Note the *MG 34* in the foreground.

Ski troops relaxing outside an earthen hut.

A reconnaissance patrol on skis can cover far more ground than troops on foot.

An effective way of delivering messages to a forward observer.

Horsepower! A German field mess, the *Gulaschkanone*, moves to another location. Here it is pulled by a team of three horses, with the smaller ones probably Russian *panje* horses and the larger one of German stock. While many think of the German army as a modern, mostly mechanized force, just the opposite was true. The *panzer* and mechanized infantry stole most of the limelight in the course of the *blitzkrieg* campaigns, but the vast majority of the German Army used horses to move its supplies and equipment within infantry divisions and artillery formations until the end of the war.

A Finnish soldier and his four-legged companion, each well camouflaged for winter conditions. Such dogs were used on patrols to find Russian partisans and sniff out booby traps.

Often the only way to move supplies and evacuate the wounded was by sled. Even *panzer* divisions used horses and sleds for transportation.

Supply personnel take a break in the woods, their cargo piled high on the wagons behind them.

A horse-drawn supply column wends its way to the front. In many instances, horses could negotiate the difficult terrain where motorized vehicles became immobilized.

Although the war was waged with unrivaled brutality between the combatants, the German frontline soldiers frequently established amicable relationships with the local populace, particularly in the Ukraine and other portions of the western Soviet Union, as well as the Caucasus, where the locals treated the Germans as liberators and actively collaborated in actions against the Soviets. Here a young boy on an equally young *panje* horse provided subject matter for the soldier sending this image home.

The German Army commenced Barbarossa with as many as 750,000 horses tended by some 24,000 veterinary troops. By March 1942, 265,000 horses were lost to death and sickness or were otherwise unfit for further service.

The sturdy Russian *panje* horses were used in large numbers, being far less delicate than their larger European counterparts.

A military policeman (*Feldgendarmerie*), known to the German soldiers as a "chain dog" because of the metal gorget commonly worn. Here the *Feldgendarmerie* is guarding a ration distribution point.

An improvised infantry position utilizing the one material that was in plentiful supply. The weapon appears to be a captured Soviet DP light machine gun. Large numbers of this effective and reliable weapon were taken into German service.

While useful, these *panje* horses could not haul artillery pieces or heavy supply wagons.

Far more elaborate are these white coats that appear to be made out of cotton and feature hoods. It may be that this is an *SS* unit as one of the soldiers is carrying a 9mm MP 35/1 Bergmann, which was used almost exclusively by the *Waffen SS*. The *SS* had its own clothing factories, and *SS* combat units on the Eastern Front tended to be better equipped for the winter of 1941–42 than army units.

An *MG 34* used in the heavy machine-gun role. The standard German gun oil froze in the sub-zero temperatures, causing malfunctions, until it was discovered that if the excess oil was cleaned from the weapons, leaving only a thin coating, they functioned perfectly.

These fortunate soldiers have been issued with the scarce sheepskin overcoat that was very effective in combating the cold. The awkward straw overshoes are evident and the soldier on the right wears what appears to be felt boots, a far more practical item of footwear.

A rather disordered dugout, although stacks of firewood are evident and a blanket covers the entrance.

Examples of the Soviet fur caps widely used by the Germans. The correct national insignia has been added to these caps.

Supply convoys adapted for winter conditions: simple wooden sleds pulled by sturdy Russian *panje* horses. These horses were much more suited to the harsh Eastern Front conditions than their larger, less robust European equivalents. However, as they were significantly smaller animals, they could not pull the same heavy loads, such as artillery pieces and heavy supply wagons.

Although both sides practiced a "scorched earth" policy, the burning of the hut was unlikely to have been deliberate as both sides prized the protection provided by intact dwellings. Numerous small-scale actions were fought for the possession of huts and small villages.

Given the circumstances, an elaborate Christmas tree is displayed in a peasant hut.
Christmas celebrations were an important component of morale for those on the front
line, and where possible, every effort was made to provide the troops with additional food,
alcohol, and small gifts.

Although this dugout does look to have been somewhat hastily constructed, substantial overhead protection is apparent. Heavy Soviet artillery and mortar fire not only preceded almost every attack, but random barrage fire was also frequently directed against German positions to keep the defenders on edge.

At the start of the campaign, relations between German troops and Russian civilians were generally amicable. This was particularly the case in the Ukraine, where the Germans were initially welcomed as liberators. Troops were quartered with families who provided them with some supplies and fresh food. As the war continued and harsh German occupation policies were instituted, partisan warfare replaced collaboration.

A variety of additional coverings over the standard greatcoat is apparent here, including camouflaged shelter quarters and blankets. Also evident is the variety of footwear, including felt boots and straw shoes.

A heavily laden patrol (or an assault squad) prepares to move out. Although most of the helmets have had whitewash applied, most of the troops are not wearing any form of white coverall for camouflage.

Mealtime in the forest. Although smoke gave away one's position, a fire was generally essential to keep from freezing to death.

Another two examples of the white overcoat with hood. Thin cotton overgarments were more easily washed—in order that they retain their ability to help conceal the wearer—than heavier items. White clothing quickly became dirty under combat conditions and lost its camouflage properties.

A prefabricated hut constructed of plywood sheets. It was intended that substantial numbers of these portable units be sent to the front in order to provide immediate shelter. However, like many other initiatives, only a handful of these huts made it to the front prior to the end of winter.

The soldier on the left, a *Gefreiter* (acting corporal), carries a map case and has been awarded the infantry assault badge and the Iron Cross, Second Class. The center soldier is wearing heavy felt boots, and on the right is an officer (*Hauptmann*, or captain) with sidearm and a signal lamp.

On watch for the enemy. The stubborn German defense, often in the face of seemingly overwhelming odds, confounded and frustrated Soviet commanders, disrupting their plans for large-scale envelopment and destruction of substantial numbers of German troops.

Most movement during the winter was on foot as wheeled and tracked vehicles were very scarce. Even during the early days of Barbarossa, the majority of soldiers marched into battle, and most supplies and equipment were hauled by horses.

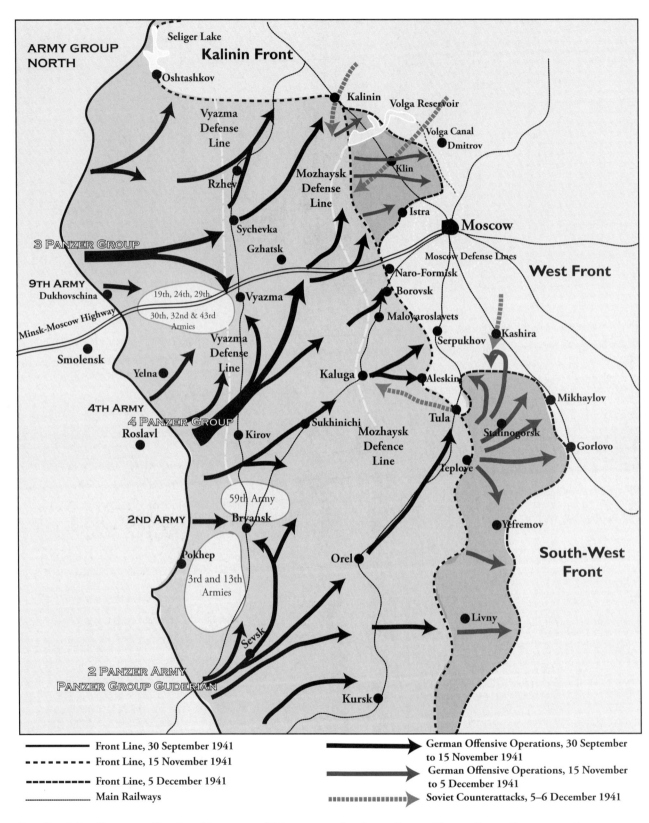

ARMY GROUP NORTH

Seliger Lake

Kalinin Front

Oshtashkov

Kalinin

Volga Reservoir

Volga Canal

Dmitrov

Vyazma Defense Line

Rzhev

Klin

Mozhaysk Defense Line

Istra

Moscow

3 Panzer Group

Sychevka

Gzhatsk

Moscow Defense Lines

West Front

Naro-Formisk

9th Army

Dukhovschina

Minsk-Moscow Highway

19th, 24th, 29th, 30th, 32nd & 43rd Armies

Vyazma

Borovsk

Maloyaroslavets

Kashira

Smolensk

Serpukhov

Yelna

Vyazma Defense Line

Kaluga

Aleskin

Mikhaylov

4th Army

4 Panzer Group

Roslavl

Sukhinichi

Mozhaysk Defence Line

Tula

Stalinogorsk

Gorlovo

Kirov

Teplore

2nd Army

59th Army

Bryansk

Yefremov

Pokhep

3rd and 13th Armies

Orel

South-West Front

Sevsk

Livny

2 Panzer Army
Panzer Group Guderian

Kursk

——————— Front Line, 30 September 1941	━━━━▶ German Offensive Operations, 30 September to 15 November 1941
- - - - - - Front Line, 15 November 1941	━━━━▶ German Offensive Operations, 15 November to 5 December 1941
– – – – – Front Line, 5 December 1941	
.... Main Railways	▪▪▪▪▪▪▪▶ Soviet Counterattacks, 5–6 December 1941

Details of the German offensive drives toward Moscow on the Army Group Center front. Some patrols even reached the Moscow suburbs, and it appeared that it was only a matter of time before Moscow fell. The reality was that the Germans had badly overextended themselves, inadequate supplies were getting through, casualties were mounting, the temperature was plummeting, and the troops were exhausted. The Soviet counterattacks of 5–6 December were just the beginning of a general offensive along the whole front.

Officer's M36
Field Tunic

Soldier's M36
Field Tunic

Standard Steel Helmet

M37 Feldmütze
Officer's Field Cap

Soldier's M34
Overseas Cap

Iron Cross, 2nd Class

Infantry Assault Badge

Wound Badge
Silver—3 Wounds

Soldier's Identity Disc

M1931 Bread Bag

Soldier's Personal Items

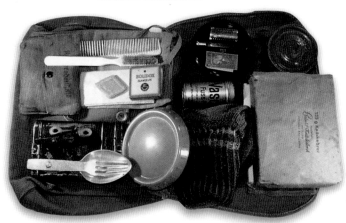

Soldier's Pay and
Record Book

M35 Map/Dispatch Case

M1931 Mess Kit

M1931 Canteen
and Cup

Leather
Marching Boots

THE WEHRMACHT

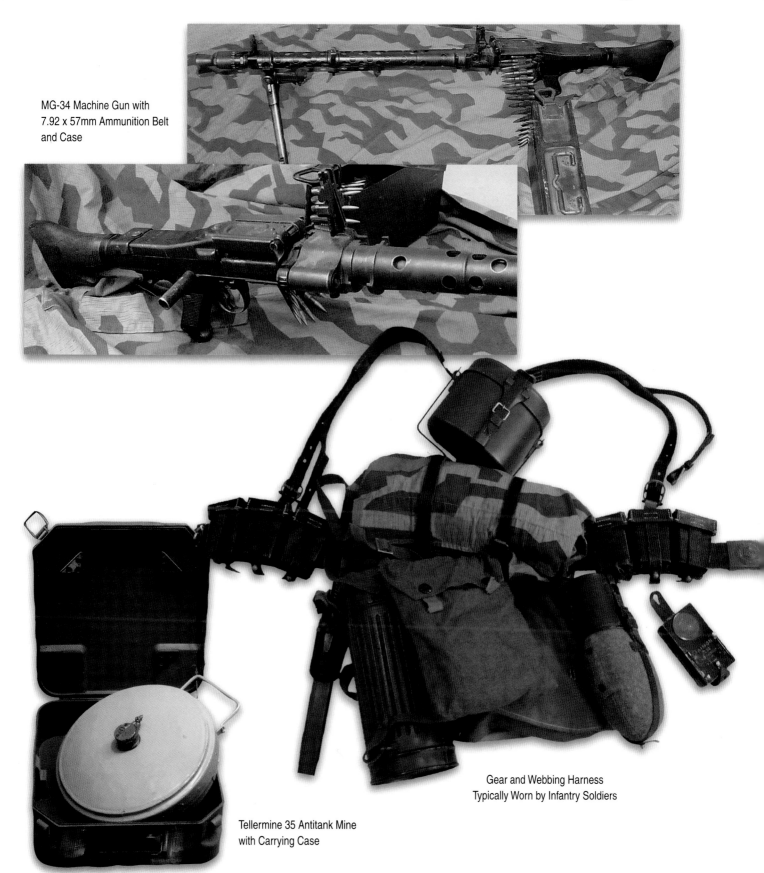

MG-34 Machine Gun with
7.92 x 57mm Ammunition Belt
and Case

Gear and Webbing Harness
Typically Worn by Infantry Soldiers

Tellermine 35 Antitank Mine
with Carrying Case

THE WEHRMACHT

KAR98k Bolt-Action Rifle 7.92mm

Bayonet and Five-Round
Ammunition Clips

P08 Luger

P38 Walther 9mm

Walther 7.65mm PPK

MP40 with Magazine Pouch
and Luger Holster

KAR98k Ammunition Pouch

Entrenching
Tool

M1928 Stick Grenade

Gas Mask Canister

WEHRMACHT WINTER GEAR

Rabbit's Fur
Winter Cap

German Helmet
in Winter White

Wool-covered
Ear Muffs

Sheepskin
Winter Jacket

Infantryman's Fur-lined
Greatcoat with Leather-
reinforced Panels

Wool-Rayon Winter Scarf

Knitted Wool-Rayon
Mittens with Trigger Finger

Enlisted Man's
Wool-Rayon
Winter Gloves

Russian
Front Medal

Frostbite
Salve

Frostschutz Salbe
WEHRMACHTPACKUNG, ZV
Nr. 0/0550/5948

Woven Straw
Winter Overboots

Winter-Issue Long Underwear

Felt-and-Leather
Winter Boots

SSH 39
Combat Helmet

M35 Soldier's
Gymnasterka,
Sappers, Infantry

M36 Combat Helmet

Wrist Compasses

Tanker's Padded
Helmet

Russian Order of
the Red Banner

Soviet Order of the Red Star

ZOMZ 6x Binoculars with Case

Mosin-Nagant Sniper Rifle
7.62mm x 54mm

RGD-33 Stick
Grenade

Mosin-Nagant 7.62mm

RPG-40 Antitank
Grenade

SVT-40 7.62mm

SVT-38 7.62mm

Nagant M1895
Revolver 7.62mm

PPD-34 7.62mm x 25mm

PPSh-41 Submachine Gun
7.62mm x 25mm

M1931 Maxim
Machine Gun 7.62mm

RED ARMY WINTER GEAR

Tankman's
Telogrieka
Quilted Winter
Jacket

White-washed M40 Helmet

Soldier's
Felt Winter
Boots

Officer's
Felt Winter
Boots

Infantryman's
Telogrieka
Quilted Winter
Trousers

In these staged photographs—note the shadow cast by the photographer, who is in the wrong location to record mine-clearing efforts—soldiers probe for mines along a snow-packed road to clear a path for an advancing *Panzer III*. The thin rods were designed to penetrate the snow and ice cap to probe for hard objects buried beneath the surface. In this case, the mines would have had to have been emplaced before the snowfall, since emplacing them afterwards would have left telltale signs of disturbance. In the winter months, mines were frequently placed on top of the snow, because it was difficult to dig into the frozen ground and any digging would announce the location anyway. This picture might have been taken in a training environment after the disastrous winter of 1941–42, since the soldiers are wearing snow uniform accessories that were only introduced later.

An early-model *Sturmgeschütz III* starts to cross a makeshift bridge over a partially frozen creek bed, while other vehicles await their turn. This appears to be one of the first efforts since the assault gun is the object of much attention by onlookers. An officer on the bridge is standing with another soldier, presumably a crewmember, who will guide the vehicle across at a walking pace. Existing bridges were often reinforced like this, since the existing wooden civilian structures were not designed to carry such heavy weights and traffic.

A train load of *Panzer III's* moves to another area of operations. Note the provisions for additional fuel by means of a bracket mount welded to the back deck. In addition, each vehicle seems to have several extra roadwheels and spare track (placed on the flat cars). These tankers are providing aerial security by means of the *MG 34* mounted to the top of the turret roof on a swivel mount. Being an air guard during the winter months in the East was a thankless task, and the additional heavy overcoats did little to ward off the cold when exposed to the elements on a moving train.

An *Sd.Kfz. 9/1* prime mover outfitted with a lifting crane is used to assist mechanics in removing a powerplant from a *Panzer III* with added frontal armor. These vehicles appear to have been assigned to the *11. Panzer-Division (Panzer-Regiment 15)*, as evidenced by the unit insignia (a stylized ghost) on the rear of the prime mover.

A *Panzer III* provides covering fire for an infantry squad as it moves through a burning village.

Panzer III Ausf. G/H's on the move. These models mount the 5cm L/42 main gun, introduced due to the lessons learned in Poland and France. However, this weapon was incapable of destroying the T-34 and the KV-1 frontally.

The *Panzer III* was Germany's main battle tank at the start of Barbarossa, during which 960 E to J models were deployed. The *Panzer IV* was envisaged as more of an infantry-support vehicle. When the superlative T-34 was encountered in large numbers in the defense of Moscow, the commander of the Second *Panzer* Army, General Heinz Guderian, commented: "Numerous Russian T-34s went into action and inflicted heavy losses on the German tanks. Up to this time, we had enjoyed tank superiority, but from now on, the situation was reversed."

In his memoir, *Panzer Commander*, Hans von Luck of the *7.Panzer-Division* detailed some of the consequences of the lack of preparation for the winter: "To be unprepared for the extreme cold had disastrous effects on our tanks and wheeled vehicles. The summer oil was too thin and the cooling water froze at once. We were soon forced to thaw water in the morning with blow lamps and procure hot water as soon as we got near a village; or else we had to leave the engines running throughout the night."

The *StuG III Ausf. C*, an infantry-support vehicle mounting the 7.5cm L/24 on the chassis of the *Panzer III*. It was also a highly effective tank destroyer, despite its low-velocity main gun.

The *StuG III* was well liked by its crews and relatively well protected by 5cm of frontal armor. Six assault gun battalions were available for Barbarossa.

Panzer III Ausf. J armed with the 5cm *Kwk L/42* main gun, the superstructure and hull armor was increased to a basic 50 mm. The 2nd and 5th *Panzer* Divisions, which were sent to Russia as reinforcements in September 1941, were equipped with the *Ausf. J.* The 5cm L/42 was not capable of penetrating the frontal armor of either the T-34 or KV-1 and 2. The situation improved only marginally when the higher-velocity L/60 gun was introduced in early 1942.

An *Sd.Kfz. 251/10* half-track, mounting a 3.7cm *PaK 36* as a support weapon, in action with an *Sd.Kfz. 222* armored car and a *Panzer III.*

An *Sd.Kfz 251 Ausf. B* could carry an infantry squad of ten and two *MG 34s.* Cooperation among the *panzers*, infantry, artillery, reconnaissance elements, and the *Luftwaffe* was exceptional.

A relatively rarely encountered vehicle was the *Sd.Kfz. 252*, an armored ammunition hauler built in 1941 to carry ammunition for assault gun units. The firm of Demag built 413 of these vehicles before production ceased in September 1941, when the role the vehicle played was assumed by the *Sd.Kfz. 250/6*.

Armored personnel carriers convey infantry across the desolate winter landscape. Even in the *panzergrenadier* (armored infantry) regiments, only a single company had armored half-tracks.

A good detail photograph of a *Panzer IV F* and its driver. The tank has been given an overall coating of whitewash to enable it to blend in with the terrain. The short (L/24) 7.5cm main gun firing special hollow-charge ammunition could destroy a T-34 at very close range. *Oberstleutenant* Grampe, serving with the *1. Panzer-Division*, detailed the difficulties of the extreme cold (in Robert J. Kershaw's *War without Garlands*): "The turrets would not revolve, the optica misted up, machine guns could only fire single rounds, and it took two to three crew members to depress main tank gun barrels, only achievable if they stamped down on the main barrel where it joined the turret block."

An *Sd.Kfz.* 222 armored car stands guard over what appears to be an awards ceremony. The 222 was the *Wehrmacht*'s standard light armored car and was issued to the armored car companies of reconnaissance battalions. Armament was a 2cm automatic cannon and an *MG 34* machine gun. Armor on this model was only 8 mm—proof only against small-arms fire.

A *Panzer IV Ausf. F* is dug out of deep snow. The ground clearance of the *Panzer IV* was not really adequate for operations in deep mud or snow, and modifications were tried to increase the ground clearance. These modifications were not successful, and the *Panzer IV* had the same suspension from 1937 to 1945.

The temporary winter whitewash has worn off this *Panzer IV F*, exposing its dark grey paint.

A very early *Panzer IV*—probably an *Ausf. A*. This photo is therefore prewar; however, it does clearly show the basic configuration of this tank. The *Panzer IV* was very adaptable to upgrading, with final variants having 8 cm of frontal armor and an L/48 7.5cm main gun that was capable of defeating most Allied tanks even in 1945. A total of approximately 8,500 *Panzer IV's* were produced.

A light motorcycle-sidecar combination, probably a *DKW 250*. The German Army used motorcycles on a large scale for both reconnaissance and carrying dispatches. On some of the larger shaft-driven combinations, the sidecar wheel was also driven, which aided traction in the mud and snow.

By November 1941, of the 500,000 wheeled vehicles that were available at the start of Barbarossa, only 75,000—some 15 percent—were still in working order.

A headquarters in a Russian village. Because of the large footprint of a headquarters, requiring communications equipment and workspace for the preparation of maps and orders, built-up areas were almost a requirement. In this image, camouflaged vehicles crowd the walls of village buildings in an effort to remain somewhat inconspicuous, especially from aerial observation.

An *Sd.Kfz. 223* radio version of the light armored car that provided long-range communications for the reconnaissance units. Issued to *Panzer* divisions and motorized infantry divisions.

A Type 82 *Kübelwagen* (the standard light personnel car), and a Type 166 *Schwimmwagen* amphibious vehicle. Over 52,000 of the former and 14,000 of the latter were built. These vehicles are from a self-propelled artillery unit.

A Horch Model 40 *Kfz. 15* medium personnel car. Based on a commercial chassis, these cars had adequate cross-country performance.

Although the specialized winter clothing places this photograph in the post–1941–42 period, it does depict the conditions that wheeled vehicles faced—in this instance, a modified Opel *Blitz* 4x4 workshop vehicle.

A specialized radio car (*Funkkraftwagen*) *Kfz. 17*. Note the chains on the tires.

It seems impossible that an engine could overheat in -60C temperatures, but without proper antifreeze cooling, water can freeze and not circulate, causing the engine to overheat and seize.

A German mechanized/motorized column. The *Panzer* in the foreground is a Czech-built 9.5-ton *Pz.Kpfw. 38t* light tank mounting a 3.7cm main gun. The dead horse exemplifies the fate of thousands of unfortunate horses in that cruel winter.

Having long and hard-won experience fighting in winter conditions, the Finns developed specialized vehicles such as this Maxim machine gun–armed snowmobile.

The large *Sd.Kfz. 8* twelve-ton half-track. Most of these vehicles were used for towing heavy artillery pieces

What appears to be a *15cm sFH18* protected by a tarpaulin is towed by a *Sd.Kfz. 8.*

A truck convoy heads toward the front line during a blizzard. The German Army never had enough trucks to satisfy supply requirements. The farther away from the railhead the frontline became, the more critical the problem.

A forward supply base with a variety of trucks and motor vehicles. In the foreground is probably a *Bussing-NAG 4500A* heavy truck with a 4.5-ton payload rating.

Motorized and horse-drawn transport struggle against the elements to make it to and from the front. Soviet road conditions even in good weather were usually marginal at best. The majority of German trucks at this time were only two-wheel drive, unlike the superb 4 x 4 and 6 x 6 American trucks soon to reach the Soviets in large numbers.

A supply convoy on a relatively well maintained road. When the ground was frozen, the dirt roads became somewhat navigable. During the spring and autumn rainy periods, the roads became a muddy morass, making it extremely difficult to move on, particularly as many German trucks had only rear wheel drive.

Cross-country personnel cars, followed by a medium truck, struggle through the rutted, muddy road that passed for a major "highway" in Russia. It was the totally inadequate road system, as much as the stubborn defense of Soviet troops, that delayed the German advance before Moscow. Not only did it take substantially longer to conduct movements, but the soldiers also arrived very tired or even exhausted.

With the roads in good condition, the advance continues. However, the vehicles cannot move cross-country. Even armored vehicles are essentially road-bound, limiting the avenues of the advance.

A 5cm *PaK 38* being towed by a medium truck rather than the standard *Sd.Kfz. 11* half-track. The vehicle in the background appears to be an Italian truck.

Loading a supply truck onto a railcar.

The tracked vehicle photos is the rarely seen *Sd.Kfz. 252* ammunition-carrier variant of the *Sd.Kfz. 250.*

Early-model *StuG III Ausf. C/D* assault guns being loaded onto flat cars. The axe carried by the soldier is for chipping ice from the running gear that could otherwise lead to a thrown track. This variant of the *StuG III* had 5 cm of frontal armor, and its very low profile enabled it to operate from ambush positions.

The low-velocity L/24 7.5cm main gun could knock out a T-34 at close ranges and at more than 500 meters using hollow-charge ammunition. *Leichte Sturmgeschutz-Abteilung (Feld) 600*, to which these vehicles may have belonged, was sent to the Eastern Front in December 1941 and operated with the *2. Panzer-Armee.*

Supplies are transferred from trains to horse-drawn sleds at the railhead.

SOVIET ARMORED VEHICLES

A knocked-out KV-2, a Soviet fifty-five-ton medium tank introduced in 1940 that featured a 15.5cm main gun and was intended as an infantry-support vehicle.

A knocked-out KV-1 Model 1941 with the 7.62cm F-32 main gun.

With its wide tracks, the KV-1 had reasonably good traction in snowy terrain, despite its weight of forty-five tons.

Truck-mounted M-8 launcher rails for the 8cm RS-82 fin-stabilized rockets. Although not very accurate, the saturation and blast effect of this weapon was considerable.

A pair of Russian T-28 tanks that have been captured by the Finns and put in use in December 1941. Designed between the wars, the T-28 was slow, cumbersome, and outclassed by more modern single-turret tanks.

A number of destroyed T-37 and T-38 amphibious scout tanks outside what looks to be a factory or workshop complex. Both models were armed only with a 7.62 mm machine gun, and the armor was understandably very thin at 3 to 9mm, barely thick enough to stop small-arms fire.

One of two British Mark V tanks on display in Smolensk. Dozens of these First World War tanks were given to the White Russian Army to fight the Bolsheviks during the Russian Civil War (1917–22). Of special note is that both of these tanks were transported to Germany during World War II and were rediscovered in Berlin in 1945.

German soldiers inspect a British Matilda infantry tank supplied to the Soviet armed forces under the Lend-Lease agreement. The slow, underarmed Matilda was not popular with Soviet tankers, and its tracks provided inadequate grip for winter conditions.

A crewmember of a destroyed Russian BT series tank lies dead in the snow as Finnish troops examine the vehicle. The Finns excelled at repairing captured equipment and reusing it.

An improved 1939 model T-26S with a cast front to the turret and more sloped hull armor. The tank is camouflaged in a disruptive scheme of irregular white stripes. Some 12,000 T-26s of all models were produced between 1933 and 1941.

A T-26S in the foreground and a 1933 model T-26 following. The lead T-26 appears to have a flamethrower attachment on the hull.

There is no chance that the 3.7cm *PaK 36* in the foreground destroyed this T-34. In fact, it looks as though one antitank gun has been run over.

BA-10 and BA-6 armored cars on the move. The turret is similar to that of the T-26 tank and mounts a 45mm gun.

The nemesis of the *Panzerwaffe* in 1941–42: the T-34/76. In addition to its other attributes, the wide tracks allowed it to easily traverse the rugged winter terrain. German *panzers*, with their relatively narrow tracks, often bogged down in mud or heavy snow.

ARTILLERY and ANTITANK GUNS

A *3.7-cm Flak 38* used in the ground role. The Germans were very adept at using antiaircraft artillery in this manner. The Allies, including the Soviets, were not so flexible.

A destroyed heavy artillery piece, probably a Soviet 15.5cm Model 1937

Another destroyed Soviet 15.5cm Model 1937 heavy howitzer.

The 10.5cm howitzer in the background is a *leichte Feldhaubitze 18* (usually abbreviated as *leFH18*), the standard light gun of divisional artillery during this period. It had a maximum range of 10.6 kilometers and a sustained rate of fire of up to six rounds a minute. The shells were separately cased with up to six charges, with the high-explosive round weighing 14.8 kilograms and the armor-piercing round coming in at 14.25 kilograms. In the upper photograph, the muzzle-brake, padded winter clothing, and the *M43* caps indicate that this photo was taken later in the campaign.

Wooden ammunition boxes.

A 15cm heavy howitzer *sFH 18* being hauled into position by infantry. When drawn by horses, the howitzer was broken down into two loads. The 15cm *sFH 18* was the backbone of the German medium artillery for the duration of the war.

A communications trench system linking the *10.5cm leFH18* with other guns in the battery. In the all-round defensive system the Germans used during the winter of 1941–42, artillery was tightly integrated with the frontline troops rather than being located farther back.

An *leFH18* battery in a very exposed position. The ground was so hard that explosives had to be used to dig trenches or gun emplacements. Therefore, when no explosives were available or deployment was required quickly, the guns were placed out in the open. Consequently, they were then very vulnerable to counterbattery fire.

This *leFH18* has been whitewashed in an effort to conceal it more effectively when not in an open firing position. Note that the crew has judiciously avoided whitewashing the area around the "kill" rings on the barrel, a source of great pride for any artilleryman. Also of interest is the fact that the muzzle cover has been attached to the gun, apparently by rope or canvas, so as not to lose it when moving.

These *leFH18s* have been located within the village proper, providing very close support. Note the use of sleds to move supplies and equipment. Although somewhat outranged by comparable Allied guns, the *leFH18* was a good, reliable weapon that provided effective service throughout the war on all fronts.

The moment of firing for the 21cm Mörser 18, the standard German heavy howitzer, which fired a 249-pound shell to a maximum distance of 18,290 yards.

Two more views of the *leFH18* in firing positions in the bleak winter landscape.

In his memoir, *Soldat*, Siegfried Knappe of the 24th Artillery Regiment commented: "Our trucks and vehicles would not start, and our horses started to die from the cold in large numbers. . . . The Russians knew how to cope with this weather, but we did not; their vehicles were built and conditioned for this kind of weather, but ours were not."

The crew of an *leFH18* rest between firing missions. The half-track tow vehicle, an *Sd.Kfz. 7* or *9*, is in the background.

Partially dug-in and with a makeshift cover, this *leFH18* emplacement offers its crew some protection.

A *3.7cm PaK 36* is manhandled into position. Even in snow, the gun was light enough to be moved by its crew, although, in these conditions, the task was laborious.

A 5cm *PaK 38* antitank gun in a prepared position. Both the gun and the revetment have been camouflaged with the application of whitewash. The *PaK 38* was a marked improvement over the puny *PaK 36* and was introduced in late 1940 after experience with French and English medium tanks in the 1940 French campaign. The *PaK 38* was capable of knocking out the T-34 frontally at 500 meters using standard armor-piercing ammunition, but the KV-1 and KV-2 were a different proposition, and special tungsten-cored ammunition had to be used.

Members of an antitank gun company or platoon that fields the *3.7cm Panzerabwehrkanone 36 (PaK 36)*, the standard antitank weapon of the German Army until 1942. It rapidly proved obsolescent in the opening stages of *Barbarossa*, when the Soviets introduced the T-34 and KV series of tanks, which were impervious to its fire. In soldier jargon, it was referred to as the *Heeresanklopfgerät* (Army Door Knocker), since its firing merely announced the presence of the gun to the enemy without being able to effectively engage the new generation of Soviet armor. Despite that, it continued to be effective against lighter armor and soft-skinned vehicles. It had a low silhouette, a light weight, and fixed ammunition. It was capable of firing up to thirteen rounds a minute.

This crew of a *PaK 36* poses along a village street in front of its horsepowered means of conveyance. Its caisson appears to have been extensively modified to allow the men to mount individual weapons, as well as items belonging to the section.

A PaK 36 and its full crew guard a roadway. If a T-34 or KV-1 appeared, either one could run straight over the antitank gun with relative impunity. This actually happened on many occasions.

The crew of a *PaK 36* dig the gun in. The low silhouette is evident, allowing relatively easy concealment.

Another crew of a *PaK 36* using horsepower to move the gun. It appears a white sheet or cloth has been placed around the gun shield in a rudimentary attempt to camouflage it.

Two views of a *5cm PaK 38* antitank gun, introduced in late 1940 in response to heavier Allied tanks. It was capable of taking out the T-34 at over 500 meters and the KV-1 at less than 500, and was supplemented, but not entirely replaced, by the more powerful *7.5cm PaK 40* in 1942.

A captured Soviet 45mm *PTP obr. 1932* model antitank gun transported on a crude wooden sled pulled by *panje* horses. This weapon was basically a scaled-up version of the German *PaK 36*. A longer-barreled version remained in Soviet service until 1945. Large numbers of this antitank gun were impressed into German service.

The famous dual-purpose *8.8 cm Flak 18/36/37* in a revetment. Along with 10.5cm and 15cm field guns firing over open sights, this was the only weapon capable of destroying the T-34 and KV-1 at long ranges. However, against the tough KV-1, multiple hits were often required to destroy the tank.

An "88" antiaircraft battery. The optical rangefinder is the 4-meter *Em.R. 4m*, the standard rangefinder for heavy antiaircraft guns. The rangefinder is served by a crew of four: range-taker, layer for line, layer for elevation, and range-reader.

A 7.5cm *PaK 40* antitank gun, a powerful weapon capable of defeating the T-34 and KV-1 and KV-2 at long range—in the case of the T-34, at over 1,000 meters. The first guns were delivered to the front in November 1941. The *PaK 40* was the standard German heavy antitank gun until the end of the war.

The *15cm schwere Feldhaubitze 18* was the standard heavy howitzer of divisional artillery for the German Army in World War II. It had a maximum range of 13,250 meters and a sustained rate of fire of up to four rounds a minute. Its separately cased shells weighed 43.5 kilograms, and the artillery piece called for a crew of twelve. Artilleryman Werner Adanczyk, who served with a heavy artillery battery, made the following observation: "At 62 degrees F. below zero, you don't think anymore. You become an automaton. You move your body to load and fire the gun on reflex, hoping it will continue to function. You don't even know any more why you are doing this; it is just a necessity to keep you moving and your blood circulating. The enemy is of no more concern."

A victim of counterbattery fire.

The *21cm Mörser 18*, along with the *17cm K18*, was the standard heavy artillery piece for the German Army in World War II. It had a maximum range of 18,700 meters and a sustained rate of fire of one round a minute. Its separately cased shells weighed 113 kilograms. Its ingenious dual-recoil system, in which both the barrel and top carriage recoiled on firing, considerably dampened recoil stresses and thereby made the gun platform very steady. Production of the *21cm Mrs 18* ceased in 1942 in order to concentrate on the *17cm K18*, with some 700 produced.

A white-washed *21cm M18* is being lowered into its firing position. The weapon could be easily swung around its firing platform by two men.

Owing to the weight of the weapon—16.4 tons—a considerable effort has been made to anchor the carriage to the frozen ground.

An *8.8cm Flak 36* being towed by an eight-ton *Sd.Kfz. 7*. The clothing and M1943 caps indicate that this is from later in the war.

A heavy artillery battery on the move with two *15cm sFH 18's* being towed by eight-ton *Sd.Kfz. 7's*. The numerous half-tracks the Germans had in service were very effective in the Russian winter conditions—once supplied with the correct lubricants and anti-freeze for the radiators.

An *Sd.Kfz.8* towing what appears to be a *3.7cm Flak M 39a(r)*. This is a captured Soviet weapon based on the 2.5cm Bofors design. Extensive use was made of captured Soviet equipment as most of it was well designed, rugged, and effective.

A well-camouflaged 3.7cm *PaK 36* antitank gun. Although useless against the Soviet T-34 and KV-1 tanks, the *PaK 36* could destroy the lighter BT-7s and T-28s. One of the advantages of the *PaK 36* was that it had a very low profile and could be easily concealed, as in these instances.

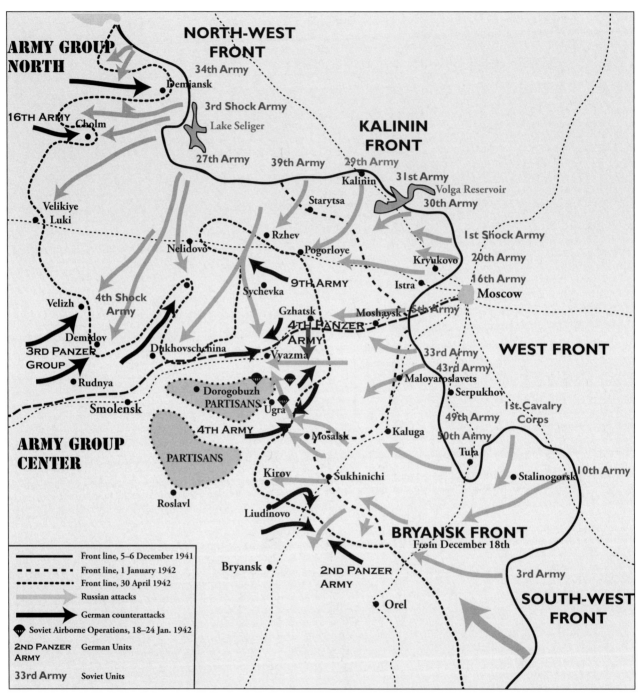

NORTH-WEST FRONT

ARMY GROUP NORTH

34th Army

Demjansk

3rd Shock Army

Lake Seliger

16TH ARMY

Cholm

27th Army

39th Army

29th Army

KALININ FRONT

Kalinin

31st Army

Volga Reservoir

30th Army

Velikiye Luki

Starytsa

Rzhev

Pogorloye

1st Shock Army

Nelidovo

Kryukovo

20th Army

9TH ARMY

Istra

16th Army

Velizh

4th Shock Army

Sychevka

Moscow

Gzhatsk

4TH PANZER ARMY

Demidov

Dukhovschchina

Vyazma

Moshaysk

5th Army

WEST FRONT

3RD PANZER GROUP

33rd Army

43rd Army

Rudnya

Dorogobuzh

PARTISANS

Ugra

Maloyaroslavets

Serpukhov

Smolensk

4TH ARMY

Mosalsk

Kaluga

49th Army

1st Cavalry Corps

50th Army

ARMY GROUP CENTER

PARTISANS

Tula

Kirov

Sukhinichi

Stalinogorsk

10th Army

Roslavl

Liudinovo

BRYANSK FRONT
From December 18th

Bryansk

2ND PANZER ARMY

3rd Army

Orel

SOUTH-WEST FRONT

────────	Front line, 5–6 December 1941
‒ ‒ ‒ ‒ ‒	Front line, 1 January 1942
••••••••	Front line, 30 April 1942
➡	Russian attacks
➡	German counterattacks
◆	Soviet Airborne Operations, 18–24 Jan. 1942

2ND PANZER ARMY — German Units

33rd Army — Soviet Units

Details of the Soviet counteroffensive from December 1941 to April 1942. The overall intention was to destroy the German Army in the East; given the limited, although substantial, forces at their disposal, this was far too ambitious an objective. Zhukov wanted the main offensive to be concentrated against Army Group Center and its powerful armored formations. Had this concentration occurred, there was a good chance that the 4th Army and the 3rd *Panzer* Group could have been encircled and destroyed. It is obvious that a number of dangerous salients had been created by both sides.

A Ju 87 Stuka comes to grief on a snowbound airfield. Note that the wheel spats have been removed so that the wheels will not jam with snow and ice. The aircraft has received a coat of whitewash and has the yellow wingtips and fuselage band indicating the Eastern Front.

Two views of *Luftwaffe* aircrew and their heavily padded canvas and leather flight suits. Designed for the extreme cold at altitude, these suits were very welcome during the winter months.

Two views of the standard *Luftwaffe* medium bomber, the *Heinkel He 111*. The canvas covers protected the cockpit and the engines from the extreme cold. The 111 was reliable and relatively easy to maintain. However, given any modern fighter opposition, it was not particularly fast at 420 kph and not well equipped with defensive armament. Many of these aircraft were used to drop supplies to surrounded German troops.

Curious German soldiers inspect a Soviet IL-2 Sturmovik ground-attack aircraft. These heavily armored machines were notoriously difficult to shoot down and were greatly feared by the ground troops, who called them "butchers."

Luftwaffe personnel show off their new winter headgear. The smart appearance of their boots and uniforms is in marked contrast to those of the troops at the front.

Ground crew/field personnel pose in front of a *Ju 88 A4* of *KG 54 "Totenkopf."*

The workhorse of the transport wings of the *Luftwaffe*, the *Ju52* served in a variety of roles due to its ruggedness and ability to land and take off on unimproved airstrips. It was frequently brought in when forces were unable to be supplied on the ground due to terrain conditions. Supplies could be air-dropped or landed, with the latter being the preferred method to avoid damage to the contents and loss due to dispersal of the parachuted items.

These troops appear to be from a *Luftwaffe* unit. The plastic face shield worn by the soldier second from the left is very unusual.

This pilot clears powdery snow from the left wing of his *Bf 109F* while a mechanic services a powerplant. While the cold did not affect the *Luftwaffe* as much in maintaining its aircraft for flight, the frequent inclement weather often prevented planes from taking off to support forces on the ground. The F variant of the *Bf 109* was definitely superior to Soviet fighters of that period.

Flying personnel brave the elements to get to their aircraft. A *Fieseler Fi 156* liaison/observation aircraft is in the background. Despite the dangers, *Luftwaffe* personnel frequently flew when even the relaxed wartime safety restrictions prohibited flight. Soviet air activity was particularly intense during the winter offensive.

A tracked vehicle tows a sled laden with two high-explosive *SC 250 Minenbombe.*

Old versus new: ground personnel work on a *Dornier Do 217,* while a traditional Russian *panje* sled moves past. Frequently, the only way to move on the ground was to resort to primitive means.

A *Bf 110C* of *1. (Z) JG 77* still in its European camouflage. The *Bf 110* gave the *Luftwaffe* very good service on the Eastern Front as a heavy fighter, fighter-bomber, and reconnaissance aircraft.

A *Ju 52* attached to an engine heater, a device to prevent engine oil from freezing. *Luftwaffe* ground crews performed exceptionally well to keep their aircraft flying in cold weather and primitive conditions.

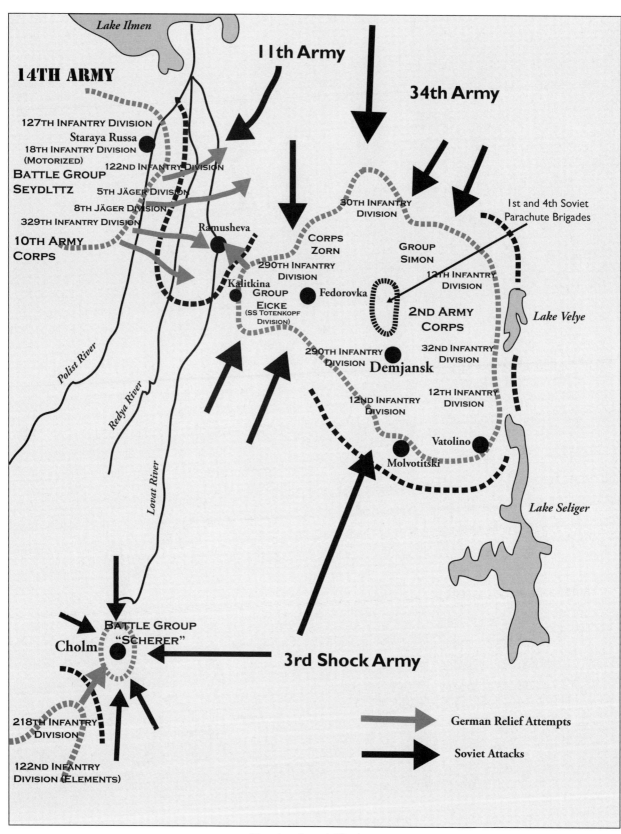

Demjansk and Cholm.

DEMJANSK and CHOLM: BASTIONS of the NORTH

Indicative of the determination of the Germans to hold localities they deemed to be of strategic importance at any cost were the sieges of Demjansk (Demyansk) and Cholm (Kholm) in the Army Group North sector.

The Soviet plan envisaged no less than the destruction of the German 9th Army and, if possible, the routing of Army Group North itself. The Soviet plan was overly ambitious given the forces at its disposal. However, if the Vyazma-Scheva-Rzhev railway line was cut, the 9th Army was likely doomed. The capture of the town of Staraya Russa was vital to the success of the Soviet plan, but part of the 3rd Shock Army was diverted to take Cholm and Velikiye Luki. This diversion of forces in pursuit of multiple goals meant that none was achieved and Staraya Russa was never captured.

The 2nd Corps and part of 10th Corps—consisting of 95,000 men in six divisions and commanded by *Generalleutnant* Graf Walter von Brockdorff-Ahlefeldt—were encircled at Demjansk. The encirclement occurred when Lt. Gen. M. A. Purkaev's 3rd Shock Army linked up with Morozov's 11th Army near Saluchi on 8 February. This was the first successful large-scale encirclement of German forces completed by the Red Army.

The German forces could have avoided this encirclement by withdrawing behind the Lovat River but, following Hitler's orders, continued to hold Demjansk against three Soviet Armies and elements of a fourth. The 2nd Corps was now holding an area of 32 by 65 kilometers (20 by 40 miles). On 22 February, Hitler designated Demjansk a fortress, to be held to the last man.

The strategic importance of these three locations was that they were located at the intersection of major roads crossing wetlands that would be impassible when the ground thawed. Without supplies that could only be delivered by using these roads, Soviet forces would not be able to hold out in the wet lowlands in the spring.

At Cholm, a small provincial town 90 kilometers south of Demjansk, the situation was markedly different. A diverse collection of units was surrounded in an area of barely 2.6 square kilometers. The 5,500 men were led by *Generalmajor* Theodor Scherer, the commander of the 281st Security Division, a lower-level division tasked with providing security for rear areas and therefore having no heavy weapons. The "fortress" artillery assets were a few 8cm mortars, a handful of 3.7cm *PaK 36* antitank guns, one 5cm *PaK 38* antitank gun, and three 7.5cm light infantry guns.

The surrounded units consisted of elements of the 123rd Infantry Division; elements of the 218th Infantry Division; the 533rd Infantry Regiment of the 329th Infantry Division; mountain troops organized as *Kommando 8*; the 3rd Battalion and Reserve Police Battalion 65 of the 285th

Security Division; and Machine Gun Battalion 10. *Colonel* Manitus, commander of the 386th Regiment of the 218th Infantry Division, was the operations officer who molded these various units into an effective fighting force. In some instances, the front line ran through the middle of the town, with no-man's-land the width of the street. One of the most contested positions was a former Red Army prison that had been turned into a strongpoint.

The Soviet high command has expected to overrun Cholm quickly, but it continued to hold out despite overwhelming odds. Artillery support was provided from outside the pocket by the 218th Artillery Regiment and Heavy Artillery Battalion 536. These units were emplaced as close to the pocket as possible. *Generalmajor* Horst von Uckermann's battle group was within 10 kilometers of Cholm but stuck in deep snow. The artillery was directed with pinpoint precision by courageous forward observers; on some days, over 1,000 rounds were fired at Soviet positions and attacking troops.

At Demjansk, Soviet paratroops were dropped into the middle of the pocket in order to create panic and assist the attacking forces, but this operation was an abject failure. Despite unrelenting artillery fire and continuous attacks, the defense of Demjansk continued, much to the frustration of Colonel General Koniev, commander of the Kalinin Front, who saw his chances of a large-scale breakthrough into the undefended rear of Army Group North ebbing away.

The only way the forces at Demjansk and Cholm could be supplied was by air—an operation on this scale had never previously been attempted. The ever-ambitious Göring assured Hitler that his *Luftwaffe* could deliver the required supplies to these beleaguered garrisons.

The supply operation was organized by Colonel Morzik, chief of air transport. At the beginning of the airlift, only 239 transport aircraft

were available, mostly tri-motor *Junkers Ju 52s,* of which 30 percent were generally unavailable due to maintenance, repairs, and the weather. Each sortie carried two tons of supplies, and as the minimum requirement for the Demjansk garrison was 300 tons daily, 150 sorties had to be flown each day. The minimum 300-ton figure was almost never achieved; initially, only 90 tons per day actually were delivered.

There were no night-landing facilities at the two makeshift landing strips at Demjansk, and when these were muddy or covered in snow, supplies had to parachuted in or free-dropped in metal containers. The number of transport aircraft was eventually increased to 600, and between 19 February and 18 May, the average daily delivery increased to 270 tons. Twenty-two thousand wounded and sick were flown out and 15,000 replacements flown in.

The supply missions were exceedingly dangerous. As there were few fighter escorts available, the *Ju 52s* flew in formations of 20 to 30 aircraft, occasionally even up to 100, and relied on their onboard defensive armament to deter Red Air Force fighters. Soviet fighter pilots were generally ineffective in shooting down the slow and vulnerable *Junkers*; even a single *Luftwaffe* fighter could deter their attacks. Antiaircraft fire was far more effective as the *Ju 52s* flew at an altitude of 7,000 feet and the Soviets set up "lanes" under the flight path of the transports packed with hundreds of antiaircraft guns. Landing and taking off was particularly hazardous as even small-arms fire could be effective; in one instance, a pilot was killed, causing the aircraft to crash, as a result of a burst of fire from a submachine gun. The *Luftwaffe* flew some 14,500 missions and 262 transport aircraft were lost, mainly through antiaircraft fire and accidents. This loss rate constituted 30 percent of the transport force.

At Cholm, the supply situation was far more desperate. Initially, the transports landed on a makeshift airfield in no-man's-land, but this was frequently under heavy Soviet artillery fire and was soon untenable. The only way for supplies to be landed was by heavy transport gliders, such as the *Gotha Go 242*, that could carry up to 4,000 kilograms (9,000 pounds) of supplies. Over the course of the siege, eighty *Go 242s* were landed. Supplies were also extensively delivered by both parachute and free drops. These drops had to be precise due to the close proximity of Soviet soldiers. There were numerous instances of German and Red Army soldiers racing each other to take possession of supply containers; vicious firefights ensued. It has been estimated that from 27 to 50 *Ju52s* were lost during the airlift to Cholm.

The success of these airlifts set a dangerous precedent as they convinced both Göring and Hitler that large numbers of encircled troops could be successfully supplied by air. This belief had disastrous consequences at Stalingrad later that year.

Demjansk was finally relieved by a specially created corps of five divisions commanded by Seydlitz Kurzbach. The attack was launched near Staraya Russa on 21 February; 40 kilometers sep-

arated the encircled troops from the 16th Army. The attacking forces advanced slowly, overcoming the deeply echeloned Soviet defense zones, and on 21 April, a narrow corridor of only a few kilometers wide had been driven into the pocket. Demjansk was then heavily reinforced and held throughout the summer as a launching point for the summer offensives.

The garrison at Cholm was finally relieved on 5 May 1942 by the former Battle Group Ukermann, now commanded by *Generalmajor* Werner Huehner. The relief came just in time—of the original 5,500 troops, only 1,200 men were now capable of combat, with 1,200 wounded, in desperate condition, lying in the damp cellars of ruined buildings and houses and with 1,500 dead. The brave defenders of Cholm had performed well beyond what was expected of them and in the end had held out for over 100 days.

In recognition of the heroic defense of these vital bastions, the German Armed Forces instituted two special arm shields: the *Cholmschild* and the *Demjanskschild* to be proudly worn by the participants in these epic sieges.

The inadequacy of the Soviet road system meant that the primary method of moving supplies was by rail. The retreating Soviets were particularly adept at demolishing tracks, railyards, rolling stock, and bridges. To further complicate matters, the Soviet railway gauge was different from the German, so track had to be converted. For hundreds of thousands of German soldiers, the train journey to the Eastern Front was a one-way ticket.

The Soviet Union is a land full of wide rivers, streams, lakes, and wetlands. Bridges were essential for both continuing the advance and bringing up supplies. The retreating Soviets destroyed as many of these bridges as they could, and German engineer units and construction crews performed remarkable feats of rebuilding and repair as shown in these photographs and those on the following pages.

A recently constructed wood and steel bridge suitable for armored vehicles.

Although Communism was a secular movement that discouraged spiritual worship, the party functionaries were well aware of the long tradition of Christian worship, primarily Russian Orthodox, that the majority of the rural population practiced. Accordingly, religious worship was not banned and churches continued to function.

A rarity in Russia: a paved road, which indicates a major city—in this instance, possibly Kharkov. It was essential for the Germans to hold the major cities as they were vital transport hubs and major supply dumps and they were defended tenaciously. It was just as important for the Soviets to capture them as their continued advance depended upon seizing these towns.

A destroyed Russian town. Even ruins such as these were bitterly contested as any cover was preferable to exposure to the extreme low temperatures and biting winds.

Even in major cities, the main thoroughfare was likely to be dirt with a loose gravel covering.

The Soviet Union was incredibly rich in resources such as crops, mining, oil, and, in this instance, lumber from its vast forests. It was the Germans' desire for these resources and *Lebensraum* ("living space") that led to the invasion.

What appears to be a very modern and well laid out collective farm. This was the exception rather than the rule.

All the larger towns had monuments to Communist heroes—usually Lenin—or a commemoration of the achievements of the "workers state." The reality of the Communist ideal was oppression and privation, although life under the tsars was in many ways worse.

A picturesque landscape, but one that presented a myriad of terrain difficulties. During the harsh winter, movement in forested or relatively open terrain was extremely difficult.

An ice hut, in this instance built to demonstrate the construction technique. To be in the open during winter was to freeze to death. Any shelter, no matter how crude or improvised, was essential.

Parachute supply canisters, the lifeblood of Demjansk and Cholm. These canisters were usually dropped from a low altitude to prevent them from falling into Soviet hands.

Trees cut down to provide fields of fire for machine-gun positions.

A somewhat crude but well-constructed bunker. The Soviet troops were masters of fortifications and could construct formidable defensive positions with exceptional rapidity.

"Dragon's Teeth" antitank obstacles outside Moscow, part of the extensive defensive rings surrounding the Soviet capital.

APPENDIX

Rank Comparisons

U.S. ARMY	RUSSIAN ARMY	WAFFEN-SS	GERMAN ARMY
Enlisted Men			
Private	*Krasnoarmeyets*	*SS-Schütze*	*Schütze*
Private First Class		*SS-Oberschütze*	*Oberschütze*
Corporal	*Mladshiy Serzhant*	*SS-Sturmmann*	*Gefreiter*
Senior Corporal		*SS-Rottenführer*	*Obergefreiter*
Staff Corporal		*SS-Stabsrottenführer*	*Stabsgefreiter*
Noncommissioned Officers			
Sergeant	*Serzhant*	*SS-Unterscharführer*	*Unteroffizier*
		SS-Scharführer	*Unterfeldwebel*
Staff Sergeant		*SS-Oberscharführer*	*Feldwebel*
Sergeant First Class	*Starshiy Serzhant*	*SS-Hauptcharführer*	*Oberfeldwebel*
Master Sergeant		*SS-Sturmscharführer*	*Hauptfeldwebel*
Sergeant Major	*Starshina*		*Stabsfeldwebel*
Officers			
Second Lieutenant	*Mladshiy Leytenant*	*SS-Untersturmführer*	*Leutnant*
First Lieutenant	*Leytenant*	*SS-Obersturmführer*	*Oberleutnant*
Captain	*Kapitan*	*SS-Hauptsturmführer*	*Hauptman*
Major	*Major*	*SS-Sturmbannführer*	*Major*
Lieutenant Colonel	*Podpolkovnik*	*SS-Obersturmbannführer*	*Oberstleutnant*
Colonel	*Polkovnik*	*SS-Standartenführer*	*Oberst*
Brigadier General		*SS-Brigadeführer*	*Generalmajor*
Major General	*General Major*	*SS-Gruppenführer*	*Generalleutnant*
Lieutenant General	*General Leytenant*	*SS-Obergruppenführer*	*General der Fallschirmjäger, etc.*
General	*General Armii*	*SS-Oberstgruppenführer*	*Generaloberst*
General of the Army	*Marshal Sovetskogo Souza*	*Reichsführer-SS*	*Feldmarschall*

BIBLIOGRAPHY

Adamczyk, Werner. *Feuer! An Artilleryman's Life on the Eastern Front.* Wilmington, NC: Broadfoot, 1992.

Angolia, John R., and Adolf Schlicht. *Uniforms and Traditions of the German Army, 1933–1945, volumes 1–3.* San Jose, CA: R.J. Bender, 1992.

Bernard, Georges, and Francois de Lannoy. *Les Divisions de L'Armee de Terre allemande Heer 1939–1945.* Bayeux, France: Editions Heimdal, 1997.

Bidermann, Gottlob Herbert. *In Deadly Combat: A German Soldier's Memoir of the Eastern Front.* Lawrence, KS: University Press of Kansas, 2000.

Bock, Fedor von. *The War Diary, 1939–1945.* Atglen, PA: Schiffer, 1996.

Buchner, Alex. *The German Infantry Handbook, 1939–1945.* Atglen, PA: Schiffer, 1991.

Burdick, Charles, and Hans-Adolf Jacobsen, eds. *The Halder War Diary, 1939–1942.* Novato, CA: Presidio Press, 1988.

Carell, Paul. *Hitler's War on Russia: The Story of the German Defeat in the East.* London: Harrap, 1964.

Chamberlain, Peter, and Hilary Doyle. *Encyclopedia of German Tanks of World War.* Revised Edition. London: Arms and Armour Press, 1975.

Ellis, Chris, ed. *Directory of Wheeled Vehicles of the Wehrmacht.* London: Ducimus Books, 1974.

Ericson, John. *The Road to Stalingrad.* New York: Harper & Row, 1975.

Fritz, Stephen G. *Frontsoldaten.* Lexington, KY: University Press of Kentucky, 1995.

Gander, Terry, and Peter Chamberlain. *Small Arms, Artillery and Special Weapons of the Third Reich.* London: Macdonald and Jane's, 1978.

Gooch, John, ed. *Decisive Campaigns of the Second World War.* London: F. Cass, 1990.

Guderian, Heinz. *Panzer Leader.* London: M. Joseph, 1970.

Hogg, Ian V. *German Artillery of World War Two.* London: Arms and Armour, 1977.

Jacobsen, H. A., and J. Rohwer, eds. *Decisive Battles of World War II: The German View.* London: Andre Deutsch Limited, 1965.

Kershaw, Robert J. *War without Garlands: Operation Barbarossa 1941/1942.* Shepperton, England: Ian Allan, 2000.

Knappe, Siegfried, and Ted Brusaw. *Soldat: Reflections of a German Soldier, 1936–1949.* New York: Orion Books, 1992.

Lucas, James. *War on the Eastern Front, 1941–1945: The German Soldier in Russia.* London: Jane's, 1979.

Luck, Hans von. *Panzer Commander.* New York: Praeger, 1989.

Metelmann, Henry. *Through Hell for Hitler.* Havertown, PA: Casemate, 2001.

Murray, Williamson. *Strategy for Defeat: The Luftwaffe, 1933–1945.* Washington, DC: Brassey's, 1996.

Niehorster, Leo W. G. *German World War II Organizational Series Volume 3/II Mechanized GHQ Units and Waffen SS Formations (22nd June, 1941).* Milton Keynes, England: The Military Press, 2005.

Porter, David. *Order of Battle: The Red Army in WWII.* London: Amber Books, 2009.

The Research Institute for Military History. *Germany and the Second World War.* Volume IV, *The Attack on the Soviet Union.* Oxford, England: Clarendon Press, 1998.

Seaton, Albert. *The Russo-German War, 1941–45.* Novato, CA: Presidio, 1990.

Smith, J. R., and Anthony Kay. *German Aircraft of the Second World War.* London: Putnam, 1972.

Stahlberg, Alexander. *Bounden Duty: The Memoirs of a German Officer, 1932–45.* London: Brassey's, 1990.

Trevor-Roper, H. R. *Hitler's War Directives, 1939–1945.* London: Pan, 1966.

Tsouras, Peter G., ed. *Fighting in Hell: The German Ordeal on the Eastern Front.* London: Greenhill, 1995.

———. *Panzers on the Eastern Front: General Erhard Raus and His Panzer Divisions in Russia, 1941–1945.* London: Greenhill, 2002.

U.S. War Department. *Handbook on German Military Forces.* Baton Rouge, LA: Louisiana State University Press, 1990.

Warlimont, Walter. *Inside Hitler's Headquarters, 1939–45.* New York: Praeger, 1964.

Zaloga, Steven J., and James Grandsen. *Soviet Tanks and Combat Vehicles of World War Two.* London: Arms and Armour Press, 1984

———. *The Eastern Front Armor Camouflage and Markings, 1941 to 1945.* London: Arms and Armour Press, 1989.

Ziemke, Earl F., and Magna E. Bauer. *Moscow to Stalingrad.* New York: Military Heritage Press, 1988.

ACKNOWLEDGMENTS

The following people deserve credit for their generous assistance in supplying period photographs taken by the combatants themselves, along with modern color images of uniforms, equipment, and weapons. In each and every case, they went above and beyond to help bring this book to life by offering their expertise and time: Pat Cassidy, Steve Cassidy, P. Whammond and Carey of Collector's Guild (www.germanmilitaria.com), Wilson History and Research Center (www.militaryheadgear.com), Jim Haley, David A. Jones, Jim Pool, Scott Pritchett, Phil Francis, and Aleks and Dmitri of Espenlaub Militaria (www.aboutww2 militaria.com and www.warrelics.eu/forum), as well as the National Archives, the Swedish Army Museum, the Finnish Armed Forces Wartime Photography Archives (SA-kuva), and a few individuals who wish to remain anonymous.

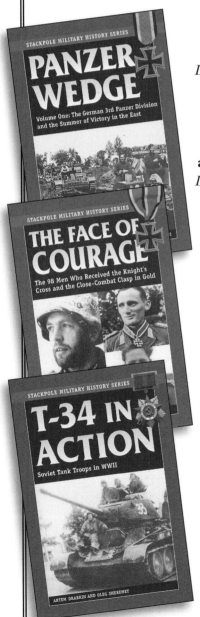